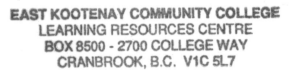

island
Encounters

island Encounters

Black and White Memories of the Pacific War

Lamont Lindstrom • Geoffrey M. White

Smithsonian Institution Press · Washington and London

Frontispiece: **Woleai, Federated States of Micronesia,
September 1945.
The U.S. Pacific Fleet Task
Force plans the evacuation of
the Japanese garrison on Woleai in the Caroline Islands. A
Woleaian Islander, U.S. Marine Corps major, and
Japanese officer engage in an
unusual three-way wartime
exchange. Sporting tradi-
tional and Japanese-era
tattoos, hornrim glasses, and
loincloth, the islander gives
information to the Marine intelligence officer as the
defeated Japanese officer
stands to the back.**
(*Source:* National Archives,
U.S. Navy.)

Cover, detail: **Fais Islanders
try out a new custom: saluting the American flag.**
(*Source:* National Archives,
U.S. Navy.)

This book was edited by Therese Boyd and designed by Janice Wheeler
Production Editor: Jennifer Lorenzo

Library of Congress Cataloging-in-Publication Data
Lindstrom, Lamont, 1953-
    Island encounters : black and white memories of the Pacific War / Lamont
Lindstrom and Geoffrey M. White.
        p.   cm.
    ISBN 0–87474–457–1
    Based, in part, on a photographic exhibition which opened March 30, 1987 at the
East-West Center, Honolulu, Hawaii.
    1. World War, 1939–1945—Campaigns—Pacific Area—Pictorial works—Exhibi-
tions.   2. World War, 1939–1945—Campaigns—Pacific Area—Exhibitions.
I. White, Geoffrey M.   II. East-West Center.   III. Title.
D769.9.L56 1990
940.54′26—dc20   90-9613

⊗The paper used in this publication meets the minimum requirements of the
American National Standard for Permanence of Paper for Printed Library Materials
Z39-48-1984.
Printed in the United States of America
10 9 8 7 6 5 4 3 2 1
99 98 97 96 95 94 93 92 91 90
For permission to reproduce individual illustrations appearing in this book, please
correspond directly with the owners of the images, as stated in the picture captions.
The Smithsonian Institution Press does not retain reproduction rights for these il-
lustrations individually or maintain a file of addresses for photo sources.

Contents

Acknowledgments

The core of this book began as a photographic exhibition that opened March 30, 1987 at the East-West Center, Honolulu, Hawaii. From Honolulu, the exhibition traveled to the Solomon Islands University of the South Pacific Centre, the Australian War Memorial, several venues in Papua New Guinea, the Vanuatu Cultural Centre, and the American mainland. We selected photographs from a number of institutions that archive World War II material. United States Army, Marine, and Navy photographs are available from the National Archives in Washington, D.C. We reviewed other American military photograph collections held by the U.S. Naval Historical Center (Washington), the Admiral Nimitz Museum of the Pacific War (Fredericksburg, Texas), and the Naval Construction Battalion Historical Center (Port Hueneme, California). In addition, we searched the collections of the Australian War Memorial, the Victoria Museum (Melbourne), the *Pacific Islands Monthly*, the Papua New Guinea War Museum, and the Fiji Ministry of Information. We contacted photographic curators at the Alexander Turnbull Library and the Auckland Institute and Museum, both in New Zealand. Japanese photographs are underrepresented in this collection. We were unable to locate official Japanese army and navy photographs. The best available Japanese collections are archived in newspaper photo repositories, particularly those of the *Mainichi Shimbun* and the *Asahi Shimbun*.

In addition to photographs stored in national and journalistic archives, thousands more exist in private photo albums and collections. We contacted a number of war veterans, both Allied and Japanese, who were kind enough to share their personal photographs with us. In general, however, nearly fifty years after the war began, the photographic negatives and positives in officially archived collections are in better condition. For that reason we have selected photographs primarily from institutional sources.

We would like to thank all the archives and collections we visited for their assistance and for making their photographs available to us. In addition, numerous people helped us in the location, selection, and interpretation of war photographs. We especially thank Dean Allard, Peggy Dufon, Cynthia Frazer, Renee Heyum, Bruce Hoy, Maj. Arthur G. King, Douglas Selleck, Col. Steven Slaughter, and Adm. Nils Wallin. Those individuals whose photos appear herein are acknowledged in accompanying captions. We also want to thank our colleagues Hisafumi Saito and Wakako Higuchi for their assistance in locating Japanese photographs.

Many others have contributed in a variety of ways to our research, providing texts, songs, and inspiration. We wish to thank David Akin, Jim Boutilier, Laurence Carucci, Samuel Elbert, Suzanne Falgout, Lawrence Foana'ota, David Gegeo, James Gwero, Kirk Huffman, Hugh Laracy, Lisa Lawson, Paula Levin, Eric Metzgar, Steven Nachman, Hank Nelson, Jim Peoples, Lin Poyer, Asesela Ravuvu, Matthew Spriggs, Masaharu Tmodrang, Gregory Trifonovitch, John Waiko, Karen Watson-Gegeo, and Marty Zelenietz. The photo exhibit that inspired this volume took shape under the creative initiative of Jeannette "Benji" Bennington and William Feltz.

We wish to thank the East-West Center, the National Endowment for the Humanities, and the Wenner-Gren Foundation for Anthropological Research for supporting our research. Finally, we are indebted to Edith Yashiki, Shuri Saigusa-Lee, cartographer Frieda Odell, and the Smithsonian Institution Press for their assistance with preparation of the manuscript.

Geographic Note

Pacific island nomenclature is sometimes complex. Many places are known by several names. Some islands and entire archipelagoes have received new names since 1945, particularly as former colonies have achieved political independence. In this book we use contemporary geographic names, but we record in parentheses the names that were commonly used during World War II. Readers may also refer to the following list to identify places portrayed in the photographs.

Current Name	Wartime Name
Belau	Palau
Irian Jaya	Dutch (Netherlands) New Guinea
Kiribati	Gilbert Islands
Makira	San Cristobal
Nggela	Florida Islands
Nissan	Green Island
Papua New Guinea	Papua and New Guinea
Pohnpei	Ponape
Solomon Islands	British Solomon Islands Protectorate
Tuvalu	Ellice Islands
Vanuatu	New Hebrides

island
Encounters

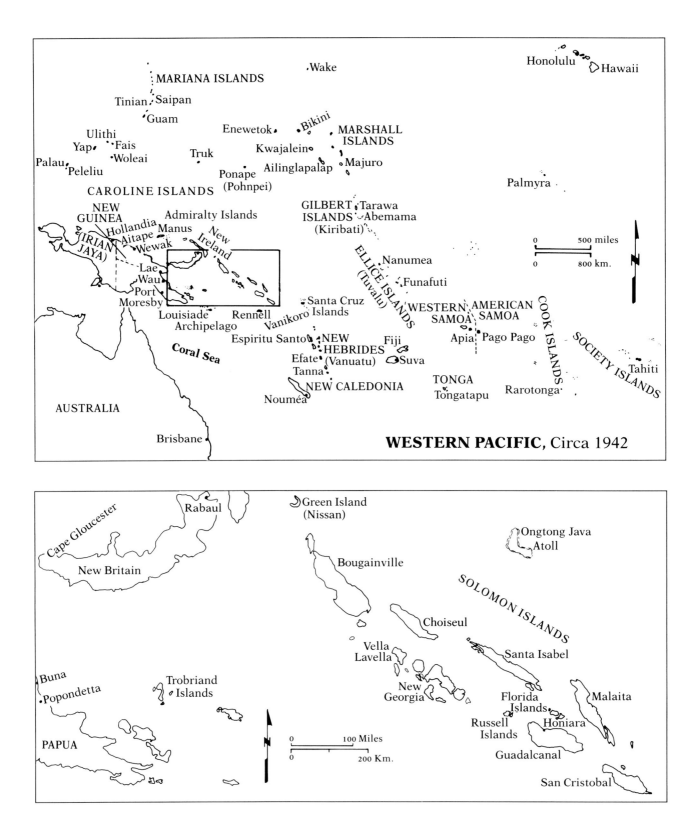

WESTERN PACIFIC, Circa 1942

1. Introduction: Posed Encounters

War leaves behind many relics. The Pacific War began in late 1941. During the next four years, the Japanese and the Allies struggled for control of isolated, far-flung island chains and Pacific sea lanes. Today, much of the debris of battle has rusted away, or is lost in shallow waters or hidden beneath overgrowing forests and jungles. Some war relics, however, have been collected for display in museums and other public places. Tourists visit these sites to catch a whisper of battle; war veterans return on pilgrimage to confront again the horror and excitement of the past (Manchester 1979). Some of the larger relics of war are spectacular. The sunken *Arizona* in Pearl Harbor, and the troop carrier/luxury liner *President Coolidge* lying off the coast of Espiritu Santo in Vanuatu (formerly New Hebrides), for example, attract numerous visitors every year.

In addition to rusting battle hardware, war relics also consist of the memories of individual servicemen and civilians who lived through the events of the war. Studs Terkel (through his book *"The Good War"*) and others have tapped this oral history, documenting the changes that World War II induced in the lives of those people it caught up and challenged. Alongside its transforming effects on individual lives—on people's bodies, hopes, and desires—the war also transformed larger social and political relations in the Pacific Basin as a whole. The war's social and political importance in the recent history of America, its allies, and Japan is obvious. But back in the Pacific Theater the war had equally telling, equally transforming effects on indigenous island peoples.

World War II swept into the Pacific islands with incredible speed and force—a force made even greater by the relative isolation of prewar island communities. The sheer magnitude of the war would be enough to ensure a place in island memories. On the island of Guadalcanal, for example, the number of Allied and Japanese servicemen who *died* on the island in six

1

months of fighting was nearly double the total indigenous population of fifteen thousand. But, for most islanders, the events that unfolded between 1942 and 1945 amounted to much more than a massive military confrontation; they marked a turning point in the history of race relations and the development of island nations.

The war came at a critical moment in the history of many island communities struggling to define their relations with colonial authorities and the wider world. The war presented opportunities for improved status and political involvement. It offered new ideas and skills that could be used to challenge entrenched colonial regimes. In areas where islanders had become increasingly restless under domineering colonial officers, the encounter with powerful, exotic, and often friendly military personnel was a catalyst for change. Memories of these encounters, and the social and political changes such encounters produced, are enduring relics of the Pacific War. It is this story, the story of massive cross-cultural encounters and social disruption, that is the focus of this photographic essay.

War Photography

A different but equally enduring sort of war relic is the war photograph. The camera, invented in the nineteenth century, was soon pointed at war. Mathew Brady's photographs of the 1860s have shaped, in large part, our impressions and understandings of the American Civil War (Trachtenberg 1985). The camera quickly became an essential component of military equipment, to be readied for battle along with more deadly weaponry, tanks, and bombs. Photographers have "shot" in every war since Brady's time (see Moeller 1989). During World War II, however, "for the first time and, so far for the last time, photography was completely harnessed to the war machine itself, an integral part" (Lewinski 1978, 95). If television provided the dominant visual images of Vietnam, the still photograph was the medium of World War II (Phillips 1981, 45).

Thousands of official military photographers, freelance photojournalists, and those civilians and soldiers who happened to possess cameras all photographed war events. No one knows the exact number of war photographs that exist today. The Imperial War Museum in London archives nearly two million World War II negatives (Lewinski 1978, 95). By the end of 1945, United States Army Signal Corps photographers alone had sent more than 500,000 photographs to photo libraries in Washington, D.C. (Thompson and Harris 1966, 564). By 1943, the Still Picture Library in Washington was so overwhelmed with negatives submitted by Army field photographers that it culled only what it considered the "best" shots from the stream, rejecting the rest (ibid., 563). Even so, in fiscal year 1945 alone, it archived 142,264 photographs. The U.S. Navy (and Marines) built up their own collections as did, of course, the Australians, New Zealanders, British, Canadians, Japanese, Germans, and even the Fijians. In the end, "from initial erratic coverage by *ad hoc* commissioned photographers, the scale and extent of the documentation had grown until . . . the Second World War was the best covered of any wars, and the photographers became veterans in the profession of photographing war" (Lewinski 1978, 95).

These hundreds of thousands of photographs freeze in time images of war-time encounters and events. We must be careful, of course, not to assume that this vast archive portrays the war's "reality." Photographers themselves recognize that images on film are not value-free pictures of raw circumstance (Rubinstein 1981, 342). "Cameras don't take pictures . . . people take pictures" (Byers 1966). Picture-makers decide what events and people are "photographable"—where to point their cameras. And picture-viewers do much more than see reality in photographs. Instead, they "read" these images by placing them within their existing frameworks of understanding. Picture-viewers must draw upon their own local cultural knowledge to determine "what's going on" in a photograph. "What's going on" in a photograph always depends as much on what's happening at the moment the photograph is looked at as on what might have happened at the moment the shot was taken.

Susan Sontag's comment about tourist snapshots applies equally to war photography: "As photographs give people an imaginary possession of a past that is unreal, they also help people to take possession of space in which they are insecure" (1977, 9). Any claims that war photographs represent reality, or *what really happened,* are perhaps more easily discounted because we *expect* these photographs to be slanted—to have functions and uses, as Sontag notes. We know that people take pictures of war on purpose. They take photographs that may be used to communicate particular stories about war, about themselves, and about the enemy:

The partisan messages of war photography are based on recurrent traumatic content. It is a content that charges two major categories of the genre: one concerned with images of pride, therefore potency; the other with humiliation. In the first group belong all views of parades, formations, exercises, assaults, as well as shots of individuals who exhibit their weapons or pose with trophies. These tend to be orderly pictures that emphasize social rigidity and hierarchy. The second list would include photographs of enemies captured or dead, interrogations, tortures, hospital scenes, retreats, refugee columns, surrender ceremonies, and executions. In such episodes, the emphasis is on the disarray of the principals, and on a social order severely ruptured or undone (Kozloff 1987, 212–13).

War photographers capture some events, some encounters on film; other events and encounters, however, go unrecorded. As such, photographic coverage is spotty. Some war events—such as those enumerated above—are heavily photographed; hundreds of cameras click. Other events take place and no one focuses a lens. These decisions and selections create empty spaces, or "silences" in our visual understanding of ourselves at war (see Moeller 1989, 15–19; Trachtenberg 1985, 25). It took seventy-five years, for example, before wounded bodies and corpses became "seeable" war images. "'No dead bodies,' Prince Albert told the photographer Roger Fenton when he sent him off to the battlefields of Crimea" (Fabian and Adam 1983, 29).

Some of these empty spaces in the visual history of war result from such orders. The military commands that no photographs be made of certain sensitive events or equipment to protect military security (Thompson et al. 1957, 405–6), and it censors or destroys any photograph that invades these protected zones (Moyes 1966, 240–41). It was only in mid-1943 that President Roosevelt and the military made the decision to allow U.S. media to print pictures of American dead, departing from policies followed in World War I (Moeller 1989, 205). The new practice evoked immediate commentary; one of the most commented-upon photos was from the Pacific Theater—a *Life* magazine picture of three dead Americans sprawled on Buna Beach in New Guinea. Thereafter, portraits of death no longer constituted one of the silences of war photography.

Other empty spaces in war pictorial history result not from conscious restriction, but from the fact that certain encounters and events are not even recognized as photographable. Pacific islanders occupied one of these spaces. Of course, the range of pictures represented here is testimony to the fact that islanders *did* find roles in pictorial history, but these were most often supporting roles, cast in subplots in the epic stories of combat being played out by the warring powers. The primary supporting role was that of "loyal islander." Brave scouts and hardworking laborers both fit this image and received significant attention from the wartime myth-machines. Villagers who suffered bombing, dislocation, and starvation did not. And so it is that photographic archives contain many pictures of war heroes such as Jacob Vouza, Sergeant Yauwika, and the heavily decorated Fijian troops, but very few of islanders who were not recruited into formal roles of scouts and laborers.

The war's photographic record, like the written record, defines and enhances themes of islander loyalty and service—to the exclusion of more complex or ambivalent moral messages. For example, the booklet *Among Those Present* (Cooper 1946) issued by the British colonial service details the heroic exploits of Solomon Islanders and Fijians who assisted the Allied forces in the Solomons campaign. The caption for a photo showing members of the native labor corps unloading a military truck reads, "RELUCTANT TO ACCEPT WAGES, the Labour Corps wished to make a community contribution to the war effort. They worked under fire and frequent bombing." Omitted from the photographic and written history of the Solomon Islands Labour Corps are the several strikes and walkouts islanders organized to demand higher wages and protest bombing casualties (White et al. 1988, 130–31).

The photographic record is also largely silent on the experiences of villagers, especially women and children, who often supported, and more often suffered, the war effort. The omission derives in part from the geographic removal of islanders from theaters of combat, but it also derives from the cultural distance that separated "civilians" and combatants in the Pacific (unlike the cultural affinities with civilians often encountered by those fighting in Europe).

We possess photographic images of encounters between islanders and military servicemen insofar as war photographers were interested to record specific aspects of such interactions. Even those photographs that capture these encounters by happenstance, in the background of a photograph focused elsewhere, present a reality that is *posed* according to a system of cultural interests and functions. "In the age of the mass media, war photographs often do not show human beings at war as they really are, but human beings at war who know that they are being photographed. When the camera is around, soldiers play the part of soldiers and victims play the part of victims" (Fabian and Adam 1983, 38). One of the most famous war photographs ever—Joe Rosenthal's picture of Marines raising the American flag on Mount Suribachi, Iwo Jima—has been reinterpreted as a posed shot (Fabian and Adam 1983, 263–64; see also Moeller 1989, 244–46). Occasionally, filmmakers recruited from Hollywood, disappointed with the pictorial impact of the real war, thought nostalgically of their film studios. Darryl Zanuck, who made the propaganda film *At the Front in North Africa,* complained, "I don't suppose our war scenes will look as savage and realistic as those we usually make on the back lot, but then you can't have everything" (Thompson et al. 1957, 400). But the fact is that *all* photographs are posed. A photographer must decide where to point his camera. Even the command "act natural" calls for another form of posing.

On the broader level, wartime antagonists posed their war photographs as a whole to tell stories about the war that they wanted told. Photography was a great propaganda weapon in World War II. "The cameraman helped fight fifth-column activities on the home front and made us anxious to participate in bond-buying and other patriotic drives. Photographs were used to weld us more firmly to our allies and to widen the gap between us and the foe" (Edom 1947, 225). Military photographers were charged with taking photographs useful for intelligence, public relations, and "documentation" (Moyes 1966, 224). They were "familiarized with news coverage and the types of photographs desired by news and picture agencies" (ibid., 218). A War Department pamphlet, issued in March 1945, sketches in comic-book form the functions of war photos: released to the press; used in public newsreels; restricted to War Department staff briefings; studied by military intelligence; made into training aids and films; published in military newspapers aimed at servicemen; exhibited to war plant workers to spur increased production; and filed in archives for "future use" (War Department 1945, 18; see also Thompson et al. 1957, 387–88). Photographs that did not serve these military functions and interests were censored and not released to the public (Moeller 1989, 8, 217).

Some photographers had their own agenda that they applied to their work alongside the military's requirements. The famed American photographer Edward Steichen, who set up combat photographic units for the U.S. Navy, instructed his men to "bring back something that will please the brass a little bit, an aircraft carrier or somebody with all the braid; spend the rest of your time photographing the man" (Phillips 1981, 34). Wayne Miller, one of Steichen's photographers, for example, was interested in the "human consequences" of war. He photographed Italian children wandering rubbled streets searching for food. Steichen offered him advice: "I think you are turning 'em out of a quality that warms the cockles of the old man's heart . . . don't be afraid to move in on close-ups—shoot *more* color—that's the only way to get national circulation" (ibid., 43).

It was this set of interests—documentation, propaganda, training, "the man," the human consequences, and so forth—that regulated the making of war photographs. The sorts of pictures we have of Pacific islanders reflect these interests and functions. We see islanders fighting alongside Americans and Australians against a common foe, or we see islanders fighting alongside the Japanese against colonialist oppressors. We see islanders suffering (usually on account of "enemy action"); islanders working in native labor corps to help the war effort; islanders being "educated" in the use of modern transportation, communication, and productive technologies; islanders being cured by military medical practitioners; islanders receiving war decorations; islanders dancing for and entertaining military audiences; islanders taking part in religious services alongside military worshippers; islanders and military personnel engaged in trade, gift-giving, and feasting together. These pictures—whether Japanese or Allied—were made to tell a story to viewers back home. This, typically, was a story of liberation, of freedom, of brotherhood, of the education of natives, or of the wonderment of islanders at the sudden advent of the modern world. As Moeller (1989, 217) notes, "Most pictures during World War II that included nonsoldiers did so to underscore the humanity of the American GIs."

Other aspects of wartime encounters are missing (Fabian and Adam 1983, 247). We do not find photographs of looting, of accidental deaths or injuries, of village bombings, of sex, of rape, of drug use, of strikes and other labor action organized by labor corps recruits in New Caledonia and the Solomon Islands. There is little photographic record of the experiences of women and children who struggled to survive while the majority of able-bodied men in a village were recruited away as laborers and fighters. Death remains anonymous, and so do many islanders. Whereas military photographers were usually careful to obtain the names of all servicemen portrayed in a picture, only a very few island names were recorded. The generic "photograph of/with natives" was enough to satisfy wartime interests.

Photographs and Cultural Understanding

This essay counts as one of the "future uses" predicted by the War Department's 1945 pamphlet. Steichen, too, in a 1945 publication of a selection of war photographs then considered appropriate for an exhibition at the Museum of Modern Art in New York City, stated, "The pictures in this book demonstrate how the camera can show what actually happened out there to those not present. They and pictures like them will take on added meaning and stature in the decades to come" (Steichen 1945, 6). Despite our doubts about the capacity of photographs in general to reveal "what actually happened out there," and despite the agenda of military interests that spotlighted certain aspects of wartime encounters while darkening others, we believe that these photographs are valuable images of cultural encounters and interaction during the war. In a recent book, Moeller (1989) has analyzed combat photos to investigate changes in American culture and psyche. If we also notice the others who stand beside or behind the Americans in the picture, we can read broader stories about new encounters and about transformations within Pacific island societies.

Photographs provide useful cultural information about the past (Banta and Hinsley 1986, 46)—about a past we presently assume and desire, that is: "the visual image will not be an end in itself but a means to enable the ethnologist to understand the wider culture(s) which 'created' the image . . . we need to understand not only each culture but the impingement of the one culture on the other" (Scherer 1975, 65).

In the case of photographs that follow, three "cultures" impinge upon one another, forming the context in which these photographs must be read. These cultures are the 1940s military societies of Allied and Japanese cameramen who took the pictures, the various Pacific cultures of islanders portrayed, and today's anthropological interests that undergird our selection of photographs from military archives and the arrangement and presentation of these photographs in this essay. Our arrangement is designed to portray the contributions that islanders made to the war effort (on both Allied and Japanese sides), as well as something of the meaning of those events for islanders themselves.

The impingement of cultures in the Pacific Theater was patently unequal. Alien military personnel, weaponry, and maneuvers had far greater effect on islanders than islanders had on the powerful militaries that unilaterally occupied whatever lands they wanted. This inequality of effect is true also of photography. We have been unable to locate any photographs that Pacific islanders made of wartime encounters and events. The vast majority of cameras pointed in one direction only. Islanders, on the whole, were photographic subjects, not photograph-makers (see Banta and Hinsley 1986, 12). The power to take photographs, of course, was also unevenly distributed among military personnel. During the first part of the Pacific War, on the American side, only officers and official photographers were allowed to have cameras.

We also do not know whether islanders ever received copies of, or even saw, many of the photographs in which they were featured. The military often distributed photographic copies widely to newspapers and to the public relations bureaus of Allied forces so that, today, the same photograph often exists in several archives. Servicemen sometimes also obtained copies of official photographs in which they were featured. Islanders almost never did. As subjects, their place was in the background. They were furniture, or exotic props setting the stage for the military's story of itself at war. International News Pictures photographer Bob Bryant, for example, working in the China-Burma-India Theater, complained when his subjects came around to the back side of the camera: "There were the curious native spectators who often insisted upon viewing the films and leaving their fingerprints. To protect his films from damage it was necessary to post a guard while he grabbed a few hours of sleep" (Moyes 1966, 241).

Although we have no examples of photographs of war encounters taken by islanders, we do have access to a different sort of island historical archive. Like other major events in the history of Pacific societies, wartime experiences have been incorporated into local oral traditions. In the text that introduces each section of photographs, we draw upon narratives and verses of songs from these oral traditions in order to hear local interpretations of the wartime events photographically portrayed. This discursive accompaniment provides, sometimes, a countering story on military poses from the islanders' point of view (see also White and Lindstrom 1989; White et al. 1988).

The third "culture" impinging on these photographic images is the anthropological. Photographic poses in anthropology differ in several ways from those found in military archives. First, anthropologists who use photographs to illustrate something about another culture generally take these pictures themselves. The photographs in this book, conversely, were taken by military photographers. Some of these men were professionals before the war; others were selected by happenstance and assigned to military photographic schools before being sent off to the front in order to take pictures of battle (Moyes 1966; Phillips 1981, 26). We rely on these men who decided, four decades ago, where to point their cameras.

Second, anthropologists commonly use photographs to illustrate or supplement written description and analysis of another culture. Although anthropological fieldwork is to a large degree a visual endeavor, that endeavor aims to turn visual experience into words—into "fieldnotes" (Scherer 1975, 65). Our focus, conversely, is the photographs themselves; the text we provide—our commentary and islander war narratives and songs—is there to supplement the pictures.

Finally, the pose of many photographs in anthropology is something commonly called the "ethnographic present." This is a tenseless, timeless idealization of a culture as a whole that often ignores hard, everyday, particular instances of social adjustment and change (Banta and Hinsley 1986, 106). Photographs of Africans herding their cattle that conceal the fact that people now must live in a wage economy, or photographs of Pacific islanders dancing in grass skirts and penis wrappers on the one day of the season they remove their Mother Hubbards and imported Levi-Strauss jeans, help maintain this idealized cultural portrayal. Military photographs of "natives," conversely, portray cultural change and disruption rather than continuity. Their posed subject matter consists of unique historical events more than enduring structural patterns. The war photographs we have selected represent historical particularities rather than cultural wholes.

Military photographs, as material for cultural understanding, differ as well from old snapshots, postcards, and other scattered photographic images that

Bougainville, Papua New Guinea, July 1945. Sergeant Lea, in charge of local recruits of the Allied Intelligence Bureau, had, according to the original caption for this photo, "a fine record of kills to his chart." (*Source:* Australian War Memorial.)

sometimes have provided material for cultural and historical analyses (see Blackman 1981). Unlike much of this serendipitous pictorial material, war photographs are extremely well documented, at least from the standpoint of the military. The negative envelopes utilized by the U.S. Marine Corps, for example, recorded the following of each photograph: "Where Taken:, Photo by:, Date Taken:, Organ'z'tion, Field No., Caption: Names L-to-R—City & street addresses, their former schools, profession and STORY OF PICTURE:." Because of this recordkeeping, we usually know the date and place of the photograph, the name of the photographer, the names, addresses, and even former schools of the servicemen portrayed. It is often possible, moreover, to take the photograph back to the island where it was made and fill in what military photographers typically left out: the names of islanders in the picture, the people on the anonymous side of wartime encounters.

This written documentation supplements a photograph's visible record of wartime encounters. "Through photographic images, a sight ceases to be a momentary impression retained selectively in memory; it becomes a stable visible artifact that enables us to seize on the deepest resources of the visible, those unremembered, often unnoticed details of material culture which are profoundly connected with the way we live, think and feel at a particular time" (Tillman 1986, 10).

War photography offers us the chance to recover the unnoticed, unremembered details of cross-cultural encounters, social disruptions, and the changing material aspects of Pacific cultures. Like so many other components of modern, industrialized, militarized life, the war brought the camera into the Pacific. Never before had so many cameras, in so many places, been pointed at Pacific islanders doing so many things.

All photographs, even the most relentlessly particular, bring to mind extensive, encompassing "narratives." We look at a picture and draw upon a bank of favorite and familiar stories to figure how that picture was obtained, and to make sense of the people and events photographically portrayed. Photographs stand in a metonymical, or part-to-whole, relationship to encompassing cultural narratives (Alvarado 1980, 8). A single photograph tells many stories, depending greatly on who looks at it. For example, a particular and unique photograph, say that of native Sergeant Lea, standing with his machine gun on July 18, 1945, at Tinian, Bougainville Island, Papua New Guinea (then Papua and New Guinea), portrays a powerful image about war in the Pacific.

All the photographs in this volume were originally posed so that they evoked military narratives of sacrifice and loyalty, stories about what "actually happens" in war. We have selected and reposed these same 1940s images so that different, more contemporary, and more anthropological themes are brought to mind. As such, we have rewritten the "STORY OF PICTURE" told on the Marine Corps wartime negative envelopes. Sergeant Lea's picture, looked at the right way, can also tell us about disruptions and change in the postwar Pacific. It can tell us about wartime experiences that not only contributed to

Allied victory but also to changes in islanders' perceptions of themselves, of Europeans, and of the future. Our story is one of the war-induced social transformations of once insular societies, a tale of new Pacific selves and others. Our captions, stories, and songs help situate the "STORY OF THE PICTURE" within a larger story about people and societies with a "before" and an "after"—people for whom the Pacific War continues to signify an important moment in cultural history. War photographs help illuminate that history.

2. Encounters

Probably the greatest impact of the war on island cultures came not from formal military activities, but from the multitude of informal encounters between islanders and military personnel who, unlike prewar colonial "masters," had little interest in maintaining a guise of superiority. Colonial authorities struggled mightily to contain the effects of these unregulated personal contacts, but in the end the novelties of war radically subverted old ways.

Wartime encounters between "natives" and military others threatened to undermine established symbols of separation and inequality. Prewar norms required distinctly different styles of conduct and dress for colonials and islanders. These differences served to maintain boundaries between colonizer and colonized. But, with the war, every encounter between islanders and military newcomers threatened to violate these boundaries and the presumption of colonial superiority. Every time an islander and soldier did the same job, ate the same food, played the same game, wore the same clothes, or addressed each other with the same nickname ("Joe" or "mate"), the established code was violated.

In Papua New Guinea, efforts of long-time white residents to reproduce prewar relations with natives were codified in a 1943 booklet written by an Australian officer for the Southwest Pacific Allied Command: *You and the Native: Notes for the Guidance of Members of the Forces in Their Relations with New Guinea Natives.* Several of the one hundred points of advice give a clear picture of prewar attitudes:

14. Always therefore maintain your position or pose of superiority, even if you sometime have doubts about it. . . .
22. Don't clasp him (the native) round the neck. Brotherhood is all right. But don't act like a twin brother. Be very much the big brother.
23. Always, without overdoing it, be the master. The time will come when you will

Top: **Pongani, Papua New Guinea, October 1942. Two young villagers look on as three Australian servicemen maintain their weapons during a stopover in their village.** (*Source:* Australian War Memorial.)

Bottom: **Espiritu Santo, Vanuatu (New Hebrides), January 1945. Two Vanuatu men converse with members of the U.S. 637th Tank Destroyer Battalion as they are given a ride aboard a new M-18 tank destroyer.** (*Source:* National Archives, U.S. Army Signal Corps.)

Irian Jaya (Dutch New Guinea), March 1944. Konga, a Kaya chief, displays customary decoration for members of three of the international forces fighting in his region. From left to right: Indonesian (Dutch), American, and Australian.
(*Source:* Australian War Memorial.)

want a native to obey you. He won't obey you if you have been in the habit of treating him as an equal.

But the Australian and American soldiers who came to Papua New Guinea to fight a war cared little for these dictates. Many servicemen objected to the petty treatment of men who were fighting alongside them and saving the lives of wounded mates.

Conflict between military and colonial treatment of islanders occurred in many parts of the Pacific. Europeans insisting on prewar codes of colonial

Dobodura, Papua New Guinea, October 1943. American nurses converse, mostly with their hands, with two men dressed in dance regalia.
(*Source:* Australian War Memorial.)

Guadalcanal, Solomon Islands, August 1943. Four Solomon Islanders, probably members of the Labour Corps, pose with Marines and Seabees who have shared or exchanged some of their rations. Even though it is likely these locals may have had little to do with the Japanese during their brief occupation of Guadalcanal, the official caption reads, "Three Marines and a Sea Bee seal international good-will with these natives of Guadalcanal, who like all of their race have turned to the Americans with an eager friendliness which speaks volumes as to the treatment accorded them by our Marines . . . compared with that of the Japs there before us." (*Source:* National Archives, U.S. Marine Corps.)

Falalop, Ulithi, Federated States of Micronesia, May 1945. Ulithian Islanders join U.S. servicemen for a meal in their mess hall. While customs of sitting at a table and eating with cutlery may have been foreign, the practice of eating together had great meaning for many islanders. (*Source:* National Archives, U.S. Marine Corps.)

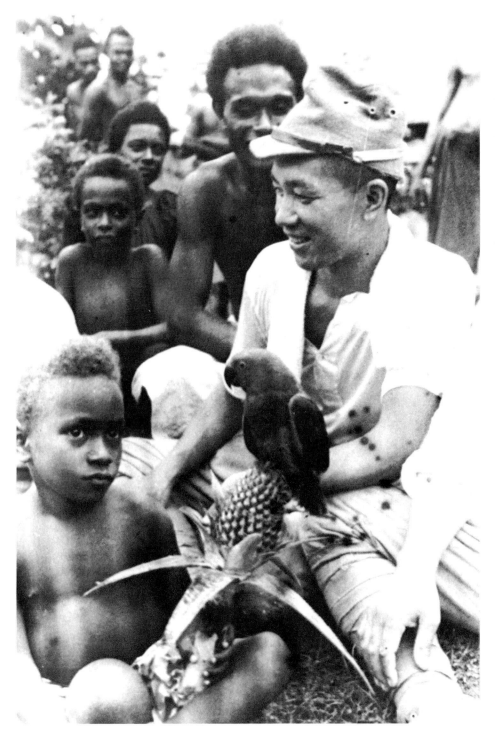

Rabaul, New Britain, Papua New Guinea, n.d.
Islanders young and old often made contact with occupying Japanese troops by bringing offerings of food. Here a young boy offers a pineapple adorned with a pet parrot. The often cordial relations established with Japanese in Papua New Guinea at the outset deteriorated as the war imposed harsh conditions.
(*Source: Mainichi Shimbun.*)

separation and superiority were particularly put off by more freewheeling American attitudes. For example, when the Fijian Third Battalion enjoyed a respite from its involvement in the Solomons campaign, they "entertained their American friends with concerts, and joined them in swimming, visiting other units, playing basketball or cricket [baseball?], and boxing. They exchanged bottles of camp beer brewed without the officers' knowledge . . . Americans' familiarity toward the Fijians caused a reaction among some New Zealand officers, who contrasted these relationships with the white Americans' attitude toward their own coloured troops" (Ravuvu 1974, 55). In some cases, the role of Americans in eroding prewar norms was even more explicit, fueled by overt disdain for colonial authority. A British officer in the Solomons lamented of the American influence: "He [the native] is a welcome visitor in their camp now, and it can be safely assumed that he will find there all the anti-British talk that he wants."

More pervasive effects of wartime encounters with military others followed simply from repeated informal contacts where the rules of European superiority were ignored. In an attempt to limit the effects of these encounters, British authorities responsible for administering the labor corps urged the U.S. commander on Guadalcanal, Maj. Gen. Alexander Patch, to issue the following memorandum (dated March 29, 1943):

It has come to the attention of the Commanding General that certain practices on the part of military personnel prejudicial to the full utilization of native labour and the control of natives by British authorities are becoming prevalent. These practices include—overpayment for services or commodities, employment of casual labour without adequate supervision or control . . . and permitting casual natives to wander through camps and military areas and encouraging this latter bad practice by feeding or making gifts to these casual natives.

The stories that are still told today by former members of the Solomon Islands Labour Corps indicate that British authorities did indeed have a problem on their hands. Despite efforts to regulate interaction between military personnel and "natives," many men who went to work on the American bases in Guadalcanal, Russell Islands, and New Georgia recall in detail their encounters with servicemen, mostly outside of normal work routines, for purposes of trading, earning extra income by doing laundry, or attending the same church services. These encounters were frequently lubricated by American generosity with military-issue food, cigarettes, clothing, and equipment. The fact that islanders profited from these exchanges was, in the long run, less important than the meaning of the exchange itself as a symbol of new types of relations with outsiders (see chapter 8). Food and other items were not only swapped, they were often consumed jointly in encounters marked by tokens of friendship, such as sharing cigarettes. Photographers interested in documenting the friendly relations between Allied troops and "natives" in particular found the act of lighting one another's cigarettes to be highly photogenic.

Guadalcanal, Solomon Islands, n.d.
Smoking together was a common means of expressing sociability. Photographers interested in documenting the friendly relations between Allied troops and "natives" found the act of lighting one another's cigarettes to be highly photogenic. Here a Solomon Islands scout has his cigarette lit by an American Marine.
(*Source:* National Archives, U.S. Marine Corps.)

Faria Valley, Papua New Guinea, October 1943.
A New Guinean (one of the "fuzzy wuzzy angels") lights the cigarette of a wounded Australian soldier being evacuated to the rear.
(*Source:* Australian War Memorial.)

Wau-Mubo, Papua New Guinea, June 1943.
An Australian soldier lights the pipe of a New Guinea carrier as he sets out along the track for the forward area.
(*Source:* Australian War Memorial.)

New Britain, Papua New Guinea, February 1944.
A Marine gives a light to a carrier on the trail from Aqualupella to Aragalpua, New Britain. The carrier still wears a Japanese coat.
(*Source:* National Archives, U.S. Army Signal Corps.)

For Pacific islanders, sharing food is a sign of closeness and trust. Exclusion from the tables of colonial "masters," except to wait on them, had always been an emblem of social distance and servitude. In contrast, servicemen from both sides found it natural and appropriate to share meals with their island hosts. A lingering impression of the Japanese among people of the Markham Valley, Papua New Guinea, was that they were not averse to sitting down with villagers and sharing rice (Read 1947). Similarly, on the Allied side, Jack Boland, a member of the Australian 39th Battalion, recalls regularly sharing meals with Papua New Guineans:

> Whenever we were with these people, at the base camps and so forth, our cooks would prepare lunch, and if there were twenty or thirty or more natives working, we'd always have them come down and share our food. This was, quite frankly, frowned upon by the local white population. They considered this not quite the thing to do at all. They were quite disgusted, and I believe they made protests (Nelson 1982, 173).

Local Europeans did make protests. A particularly vocal objection was provoked by a breach of one of the most taboo boundaries: that between black Melanesian men and white women. When a photograph appeared in an Australian newspaper showing the American film star Carol Landis (on tour in Papua New Guinea) lighting the cigarette of a virile young Papuan, an incensed white colonial was prompted to write to the *Pacific Islands Monthly* (September 1944): "Knowing the native, it will take a lot to convince me that

Halavo, Nggela (Florida Islands), Solomon Islands, September 1943.
At Halavo Seaplane Base, islanders teach black American Seabees (in shirts) how to make thatch for shading cooler barracks.
(*Source:* National Archives, U.S. Navy.)

Nggela (Florida Islands), Solomon Islands, September 1943. Three Seabees (two of them black Americans) barter with local traders for fruit, betel nut, walking sticks, and grass skirts.
(*Source:* U.S. Naval Construction Battalion Center.)

Port Moresby, Papua New Guinea, November 1944. Anthropologist and Lt. Col. Camilla Wedgewood entertains local children with string figures.
(*Source:* Australian War Memorial.)

the 'coon' in the picture has his eye on the match. If this sort of thing is allowed by Canberra officials, then what respect is a white woman going to receive from natives when later women are permitted to return to the Territory?"

As in the European colonies swept up in the war, the events of World War II also altered the position of islanders in the Japanese territories of the northern Pacific. Particularly in Palau (today also known as Belau), seat of the Japanese *Nanyocho* administration, the outbreak of hostilities occasioned a rethinking of native policies. Whereas islanders and Japanese had been strictly separated, the authorities redefined islanders as members of the "nation of the Emperor of Japan," opened up new avenues of advancement in the civil service, and included them in patriotic and religious rituals once restricted to Japanese. The unprecedented wartime needs of previously "omnipotent" colonial powers were not lost on Pacific islanders. Many responded by stepping into the role of ally, capable of giving critical support. Photographs help document the wide range of ways in which this role was enacted, ranging from combatant to laborer to contributor of war funds.

Irian Jaya (Dutch New Guinea), March 1944.
A young Kaya boy gives an Australian soldier a lesson in native weaponry as an Indonesian (Dutch East Indies) soldier and a local man look on.
(*Source:* Australian War Memorial.)

The absurdity of petty distinctions required by prewar colonial practices became most obvious in combat situations where islanders were brought into the ranks of military units to perform many of the same duties as overseas troops (see chapter 3). As George Maelalo, one of a small brigade of Solomon Islanders who fought with U.S. Marines right through the Guadalcanal and Bougainville campaigns, noted, "When you are dug in under fire, it

Guadalcanal, Solomon Islands, February 1944. Originally captioned, "Marine monkey-shines," an American Marine plays at carrying a basket, native style.
(*Source:* National Archives, U.S. Marine Corps.)

Guadalcanal, Solomon Islands, August 1943. Solomon Islander Matthew Lova "soundly whips" Pfc. William Fey in a game of checkers as others look on in amusement.
(*Source:* National Archives, U.S. Marine Corps.)

Dumpu, Papua New Guinea, November 1943.
An Australian soldier acting as bookmaker for the annual Melbourne Cup horse race explains the practice to a New Guinean.
(*Source:* Australian War Memorial.)

Majuro, Marshall Islands, May 1945.
A ventriloquist and his two charges entertain Marshall Islanders as part of a visit by Marine entertainers.
(*Source:* National Archives, U.S. Navy.)

doesn't matter whether you are white, brown, black, or red. Everyone was 'Charlie' or 'Joe.'" The recollections of Sir John Guise of Papua New Guinea give vivid testimony to the kind of camaraderie often engendered in the life-and-death scenes of war:

I was sent out to rescue some Australian soldiers that were on rafts between Goodenough Island and Cape Frere. Two very seriously wounded Australian solders; very very young, I would say around seventeen. They were mortally wounded. You could smell them; gangrene had set in. Both of them lay on my lap, one here, the other there. They asked me, 'Brush my hair, please.' So I brushed his hair and they were crying. They were talking about 'Daddy, Mummy.' It was very sad. I knew they would not live. As soon as we came through East Cape they held me, both of them held me. They were finished, dead. One could not help but feel that I was like them and they were like me. Just ordinary human beings. I mean the friendship was bound, if I may use that term, on the battlefield of blood; and if friendship is bound on the battlefield, then it is difficult to eradicate (Nelson 1982, 172).

The sight of black American soldiers wearing the same uniforms and performing many of the same tasks as white soldiers carried a powerful message for black (Melanesian) islanders. Approximately two hundred thousand black U.S. military personnel served in the Far East and the Pacific. Since many were in service units (quartermaster, transportation, Seabees), they had considerable contact with island labor forces. Apparently the segregation of American forces left much less of an impression on island memories than the obvious abilities and achievements of American blacks (but cf. Koch

Saipan, Northern Mariana Islands, June 1944. A sixty-one-year-old Chamorro woman on Saipan looks over photographs shown by a U.S. Marine. (*Source:* National Archives, U.S. Marine Corps.)

Right: **Guadalcanal, Solomon Islands, October 1943. Alex Kwaisufu, a private in the Solomon Islands Labour Corps, observes Lt. Charles Schuman of New York filling out an absentee voting ballot. This artfully posed photo represents, in an explicit and formal way, a process of political communication that went on constantly in implicit and informal ways between islanders and military others.**
(*Source:* National Archives, U.S. Army Signal Corps.)

1978, 30; Weeks 1987). Jonathan Fifi'i remembers from his experiences in the Solomon Islands Labour Corps: "We saw the black soldiers there, and they all wore shirts, and they wore trousers. And their job was to work just like the white soldiers . . . they were really great people! Any kind of thing that the whites did, they could do it too. They knew how to do carpentry, and they knew how to write. And they were the people we worked together with" (White et al. 1988, 224).

Similar sentiments are echoed throughout the Melanesian region where dark-skinned islanders had learned to regard color differences as an inevitable sign of inequality. The more egalitarian relations experienced in interactions with Australian and American soldiers were epitomized in the revelation that some of these were black. Comments by Sir John Guise mirror those of Fifi'i quoted above and many other Melanesians:

I think the attitude of the Australian soldiers, together with American soldiers, made a tremendous impact psychologically. Because here we saw a different type of white people who were friendly, who shared things with us. There was no paternalistic outlook from them, you know. And when the coloured Americans came along, the negroes came along, we said, 'Well, we didn't know that a black man could be a captain, a black man could be a colonel, a black man could be a major'. This had a tremendous effect, it made us think that the brown and black person were just as good as the white people, and that the white people, the brown people and black people were all equals (Nelson 1982, 173).

Some of the greatest resentments were created by colonial authorities attempting to reimpose prewar codes of dress and interaction after the war ended. For example, a Solomon Islander, Sam Anofou, was jailed for two days for wearing pants while serving in the Solomon Islands Labour Corps. Even though he had been issued the trousers as a member of the Defence Force, they were not permitted in the Labour Corps. British authorities had organized these on the model of plantation labor, requiring workers to wear waistcloths and prohibiting shirts and pants. Anofou was unlucky enough to have presumed that he would be entitled to continue to wear long pants as a former member of the Defence Force. A similar problem emerged in Papua New Guinea when soldiers trained in a unit outfitted with regular uniforms were transferred to the Papua Infantry Battalion and required to wear only waistcloths. Islanders who had already proved themselves in fighting on the Kokoda Trail were outraged and momentarily rebelled at the demeaning return to the plantation dress code.

Both participants in wartime encounters—islanders and outsiders (whether Allies or Japanese)—learned a great deal about one another in a short time. Other than the necessities of learning about modern warfare and work routines, islanders acquired a much fuller understanding of the culture of Westerners and Japanese, including more knowledge about their music, food, sports, politics, and language. For their part, islanders taught curious newcomers (admittedly, many were not curious) about "custom": how to dance, weave thatch, make fire with sticks, and make string-figures, as well

Opposite: **Fais, Federated States of Micronesia, January 1945.**
Four Fais men sort newly acquired American money with advice from U.S. Marines. After three decades of Japanese colonial rule, during which their island was extensively mined for phosphate, American occupation implied new cultural, economic, and political practices. Note the rising sun tattoo, patterned after the Japanese motif, on the second islander from the right.
(*Source:* National Archives, U.S. Navy.)

Kiribati (Gilbert Islands), December 1943.
Captioned "Native goes Marine," this photo gives an indication of the speed with which many islanders picked up the manners and customs of military occupiers. Attired in navy cap and grass skirt (probably for sale), this Kiribati boy (named "Sam") gives Pvt. Harley Markley a snappy salute. The residents, who had just gotten used to bowing to Japanese military, quickly adapted to saluting the Americans.
(*Source:* National Archives, U.S. Marine Corps.)

as how to fight in the jungle. Whereas islanders' knowledge of Western culture had been acquired almost entirely through the agency of Christian missions prior to the war, wartime experiences offered access to other, more secular dimensions of Western society. In many areas, villagers showed open delight at new ideas and practices suddenly available to them. A Catholic missionary on Buka, where the Japanese established one of their strongholds in Melanesia, lamented, "The children learned Japanese songs much quicker than they did my hymns" (Lincoln 1979, 6).

One area of secular "education," for better or worse, was that of sexual activity. Although many servicemen never saw native women on the islands, where villages were off limits and many residents went into hiding in interior regions, those in other areas, particularly around rear-area bases, frequently pursued sexual contacts with island women. The Pacific War was responsible for the introduction of new sexual practices and, in some areas, of prostitution and venereal disease. The latter problem reached alarming proportions around some of the large U.S. bases, where U.S. Army and Navy medical corps worked mightily to contain sexually transmitted diseases. In Tonga where, contrary to prewar norms, U.S. Navy personnel lived openly with Tongan women out of wedlock, women judged to be of "loose character" were periodically rounded up for diagnosis and treatment.

Elsewhere, the war engendered opportunities for education of a more positive sort—education that laid the foundation for the eventual severing of colonial ties. In the early phase of the war, for example, the Japanese in-

Papua New Guinea, n.d.
The Japanese were in Bougainville and other parts of New Guinea from early 1942 until the end of the war in 1945. They established schools in several areas, teaching many young islanders the fundamentals of Japanese language.
(*Source: Asahi Shimbun.*)

Irian Jaya (Dutch New Guinea), n.d.
Children play at sumo wrestling as their Japanese tutors look on.
(*Source: Asahi Shimbun.*)

Guam, March 1945.
Just one month before being
killed by a burst of machine-
gun fire on a small island off
the coast of Okinawa, famed
war correspondent Ernie Pyle
enjoys a happy moment with
local children.
(*Source:* National Archives,
U.S. Navy.)

creased opportunities for advanced education in Micronesia, and set up elementary schools in Bougainville and along the north coast of New Guinea. Michael Somare, who became the first prime minister of Papua New Guinea, remembers that he had his first year of schooling from the Japanese who occupied his area in 1942 (Somare 1970). In Palau, where people had access to Japanese education during thirty years of colonial rule, a song composed at the end of the war laments their departure:

> We won't forget you good people [Japanese]
> who were our teachers for 30 years,
> My favorite *sakura* [nostalgic song].
> Our relationship with you has ended.
> We don't know which direction to go next.

Pago Pago, American Samoa, December 1944.
The color guard of the Samoan Fitafita Guard stand in front of their barracks.
(*Source:* National Archives, U.S. Navy.)

3. Combat

Even as the war was causing hardship and suffering, it presented Pacific islanders with new opportunities. One of the most significant of these was the possibility of serving in combat roles with Allied and Japanese forces. On many islands where traditional warrior status had lain dormant since colonial pacification, taking up arms and fighting alongside the major world powers enhanced self-esteem and permanently changed views of the outside world. In all parts of the Pacific, whether the British Solomon Islands or Japanese-controlled Micronesia, the advent of hostilities led colonial authorities to discover "latent" abilities in the native populations they governed. Men previously regarded as fit only for plantation labor were suddenly thrust into training for hastily formed Defence Corps. In a statement revealing of prewar colonial attitudes, a British coastwatcher observed, "They revealed qualities of body and mind which had not been suspected prior to the war and carried out tasks which had previously been thought to be beyond their capacities" (Horton 1970, 226).

In the Japanese territories of Micronesia, where islanders had been schooled for more than twenty years in the Japanese educational system, the war occasioned new expressions of identification with the empire. These sentiments were already evident in 1937 when some Micronesians petitioned the Japanese government for citizenship. Islanders from Rota, Saipan, and Pohnpei requested that they be allowed to fight as Japanese in the escalating China war. The outbreak of World War II fostered greater Japanese recognition of islander aspirations, leading to the organization of formal military and support units in several areas. Mesubed Michael, member of a Palauan "survey group" (*Chosatai*) sent to Irian Jaya (Dutch New Guinea), wrote a song capturing his sense of new identity. The song was written in Japanese and modeled on a prewar Japanese patriotic song:

Liverpool camp, Australia, n.d.
Volunteers of the Bataillon du Pacifique pose for a group photo one Sunday, possibly after church. Among the New Caledonians, Australians, and Tahitians is the son of the Tahitian postwar leader Pouvanaa, Marcel a Oopa (right, front), decorated repeatedly for his bravery serving with the Tahitian unit in North Africa and Italy.
(*Source:* Le Memorial Polynesien.)

Port Moresby(?), Papua New Guinea, January 1941.
Papuan Infantry, members of the Pacific Islands Regiment on parade. These troops were to play a critical role in the early phase of the war, ultimately stopping the Japanese advance southward toward Australia in difficult fighting on the Kokoda Trail.
(*Source:* Australian War Memorial.)

Far from our home
Palauan youth advance toward the south;
Some sixty members of a survey group;
On our shoulders rests the name of Palau,
the opportunity for us to devote ourselves
to the Emperor's country, Japan, has come.

Military Units

During the war, formal military units were organized in nearly every colony and territory. In areas away from the front lines, police forces and militias were expanded and put through accelerated training. For example, in Vanuatu (then the New Hebrides), more than two hundred men, mostly from the island of Malekula, joined the New Hebrides Defence Force. In American Samoa, not only was the U.S. Navy's indigenous Fitafita guard expanded, hundreds of Samoans were for the first time allowed to volunteer for military service, either as Navy or Marine Corps Reserve. The recruitment of a greater

New Britain, Papua New Guinea, November 1944. Members of B Company, First New Guinea Infantry Battalion are ferried toward Pomio Village where they were to establish their headquarters. Standing with knife is Company Sergeant Major Kube.
(*Source:* Australian War Memorial.)

number of islanders into military roles, with many given the ranks of corporal and sergeant, transformed expectations on both sides of the colonial relationship. As put succinctly in the film *Angels of War* about Papua New Guinea, "When you give a 'boy' a gun, he isn't a boy anymore." Although the prestige of the European colonial powers suffered greatly because of reversals at the outset of the war, their weakened position offered islanders the opportunity to assert themselves as allies capable of giving critical support to their prewar "masters." In the French colony of Tahiti, Polynesian villagers turned out in droves requesting to be sent to Europe to help de Gaulle liberate the "mother country." Enlistment in Papeete had to be stopped within a week due to a shortage of uniforms and rifles (Danielsson and Danielsson 1977, 19).

In Papua New Guinea and the Solomon Islands, where the most sustained jungle fighting occurred over a period of years, both sides recruited local scouts and trained island military units. The Allies recruited more than thirty-five hundred Papuans and New Guineans into the Pacific Islands Regiment, made up of the Papuan Infantry Battalion (PIB), and the First and Second New Guinea Infantry Battalions. The first company of the Papuan Infantry Battalion was raised in June 1940, and was soon thrown into the breach when the Japanese landed at Buna in 1942. These men played an important role in stopping the Japanese advance southward toward Port Moresby across the Kokoda Trail. At that stage, recruits were "enlisted" on the trail and their training consisted of bearing arms in action. Despite their lack of training, many soon distinguished themselves as decorated veterans (Barrett 1969).

Papua New Guinea, n.d. Local volunteers who served with the Japanese forces in New Guinea raise their rifles for a group photo.
(*Source: Mainichi Shimbun.*)

Although newcomers in Papua New Guinea, the Japanese also wasted no time in inducting islanders into military service and labor groups. The landing of the Japanese posed a dilemma for New Guineans in occupied areas: should they remain loyal to the Australians who had fled in disarray, perhaps never to return, or throw their lot in with the new Japanese colonial presence? Many communities were divided, sometimes along the lines of traditional rivalries or animosities. However, the Japanese offer to provide education and training was attractive to many islanders. Michael Somare recalls in his autobiography (1975) that, in his home area around Wewak, the Japanese gave military training to young boys from twelve to fifteen. Adult men were recruited into the Japanese police force, the *kempeitai*, with some given officer rank. Where both the Australians and Japanese enlisted recruits, villagers sometimes found themselves on opposite sides of military encounters. On Bougainville, not only were New Guineans fighting New Guineans, but Fijians and Solomon Islanders lined up with the Allies against the Japanese and their island recruits.

Encouraged by their chiefs and staunchly loyal to the British cause, more than two thousand Fijians joined new military battalions. Ratu Sir Lala Sukuna, a paramount chief, urged recruitment with the view that "Fijians will never be recognized unless our blood is shed first." And shed blood they did, during months of arduous jungle fighting in the Solomon Islands and Bougainville. While unfamiliar with modern warfare at first, the fighting awakened pre-Christian traditions of warfare, including in one instance the practice of cannibalism:

Viliame Lomasalate of No. 5 Platoon ran forward, dragged two dead Japanese toward his NCOs and was going to cut them into portions to be shared among the men when the NCOs intervened. They stopped him only after overpowering him in a wres-

Papua New Guinea, 1943. Three members of a Papuan Infantry unit at rifle practice. (*Source:* Australian War Memorial.)

Papua New Guinea, 1943.
An infantryman who received
a military medal for working
behind enemy lines displays
his marksmanship with an
Owen gun on a target range.
(*Source:* National Archives,
U.S. Army Signal Corps.)

tling match. He had already told some of his company before they embarked for the Solomons that the first enemy to be caught or killed by the unit would be shared among the various *yavusa* [clans] participating in the battle (Ravuvu 1974, 53).

The image of loyal and fierce jungle fighters captured the imagination of Allied troops (and media), and the reputation of Fijian soldiers for bravery spread widely. An American sailor wrote in his diary, "We also have some Fiji Islanders fighting here. The Japs are afraid of them. They love to cut the Japs up. One Fiji had 40 Jap dog tags which he had taken from the Japs he killed" (Fahey 1963, 46). An OSS report on conditions on Guadalcanal in December 1942 notes, "Informant told of several incidents where natives had gone into the marshes and captured Japanese soldiers bringing them back to the Marine headquarters, where they 'sold' them to the Marines in exchange for a package of cigarettes."

The Japanese, for their part, also recruited loyal islanders from distant islands to help with their New Guinea campaign—in their case from their dominions in Micronesia. Although small in numbers, these recruits played significant roles and took grievous losses. A group of twenty Pohnpeians called the *Kessitihai* was recruited in May 1942 and sworn to die for Japan. Most of them did; only three of the twenty returned from fighting in New Guinea where they were sent in July 1942. Termed the Pohnpeian "death band" by a Japanese veteran who knew them (Watakabe 1972), these men were first sent

Below, left: **Bougainville, Papua New Guinea, March 1945.**
Three platoons of the First New Guinea Infantry Battalion kept track of numbers of enemy killed. Here a soldier updates the "scoreboard." The original caption to this picture read, "Keen competition exists between platoons on the number of Japanese killed."
(*Source:* Australian War Memorial.)

Below, right: **Singorkai, Papua New Guinea, March 1944.**
A soldier of the Papuan Infantry Battalion stands guard over four Japanese prisoners.
(*Source:* Australian War Memorial.)

to Rabaul in New Guinea, and then split up and assigned to various Japanese units later annihilated in the fighting around Buna. The recruitment of the Pohnpeian unit signaled a rise in islander status. Although it was prohibited to sell alcohol to "natives" at that time, Watakabe (1972, 208) recalls that the government sponsored a farewell party for the recruits that included "banquet drinking" over the course of two days and nights. When it was finished, "those young men, who had steeped in liquor for the first time in their lives, felt as if they had been let free from their class and become true Japanese soldiers."

Palauans also volunteered for service with the Japanese army. "Survey groups" (*Chosatai*) of sixty men each were sent to New Guinea where they could apply their knowledge of the tropics in providing logistic support (Higuchi 1984). In addition, twenty-nine Palauans formed a military unit (*Teishintai*, "devoting one's life") that served with the Japanese in Irian Jaya. Of these, seven men were killed and are buried at Manokwari, Irian Jaya. The *Teishintai* who returned to Palau, together with new recruits, were selected

New Georgia, Solomon Islands, July 1943.
Fijian soldiers pose with their weapons while taking a break during the fighting around Munda, New Georgia. Fijian military units included New Zealanders, Tongans, British, and even Solomon Islanders.
(*Source:* National Archives, U.S. Army Signal Corps.)

New Georgia, Solomon Islands, December 1943. Fijians sing as they ride a barge at the start of a patrol. (*Source:* National Archives, U.S. Navy.)

Guadalcanal, Solomon Islands, December 1942. Three Solomon Islands scouts stand at attention with a grinning U.S. Marine wearing Japanese souvenirs. Most of those who had trained as police prior to the war served as scouts with the Solomon Islands Defence Force. (*Source:* National Archives, U.S. Navy.)

**Guadalcanal, Solomon
Islands, November 1942.
At a time when the battle for
Guadalcanal was still raging,
Solomon Islands scouts guide
a U.S. Marine raider battal-
ion into the island's rugged
hills.**
(*Source:* National Archives,
U.S. Marine Corps.)

Buna area, Papua New Guinea, November 1942. United States Army officers look on intently as a member of the local police constabulary draws a map showing the positions of Japanese forces during the Allied drive on Buna. Intelligence provided (to both sides) by islanders familiar with local terrain and enemy troop deployments was often a critical factor in military operations.
(*Source:* National Archives, U.S. Army Signal Corps.)

U.S. Submarine *Dace*, March 1944.
Front row (l. to r.): Mariba, Yali, McNicol, Buka, Mas. European and New Guinean members of a coastwatching party pose on board the submarine that landed them in the Hollandia (Jayapura) area to reconnoiter prior to Allied landings. Only seven of these twelve survived the aborted mission. One of them, Yali, went on to become the leader of a prominent political (cargo) movement after the war.
(*Source:* Australian War Memorial.)

**Seghe, New Georgia, Solo-
mon Islands, March/April 1943.
Members of the coastwatching group serving under
Donald Kennedy ("Kennedy's
Army") practice sighting
rifles at their base in the
Western Solomons. Note Japanese helmets, indicative of
the source of most of this
unit's equipment.**
(*Source:* Col. Michael Currin
[USMC, ret.].)

to serve as guerrillas in the defense of Palau. They were assigned to suicide missions against the U.S. Marines in which they were to strap bombs on their backs and rush the Marine lines. Fortunately, this plan was never carried out.

The longest war journeys were undertaken by the Maori Battalion and the Bataillon du Pacifique (made up of Tahitians and New Caledonians)—both of which fought with the Allies in Europe. The service of the Maori Battalion (28th Battalion of the Second New Zealand Division) in World War II is regarded as a benchmark in the Maori community's revitalization in the twentieth century. This battalion took more casualties in the course of action in Italy than any other unit in the New Zealand Expeditionary Force (Phillips 1957). The record of the three hundred Polynesian volunteers in the Bataillon du Pacifique is similarly distinguished. One third of them were killed in action in North Africa, Italy, France, and Germany.

In the Solomon Islands, preparations for war began with the formation of the Solomon Islands Defence Force in 1937. An initial plan to recruit only Europeans and Chinese was quickly abandoned, and Solomon Islanders serving in the police force were inducted into the Defence Force and given military training. Touted as the "youngest combatant unit in the [British] Empire," the SIDF comprised less than 400 recruits at peak strength. When the British administration evacuated the capital at Tulagi, these recruits formed the primary support for European coastwatchers who remained behind Japanese lines to provide critical strategic information for the Allies. With the advance of U.S. troops in the Guadalcanal, New Georgia, and Bougainville campaigns, members of the SIDF also fought alongside U.S. Marine and Army units. While available statistics for such a dispersed force are sketchy, one coastwatcher tallied the record of the SIDF as 350 Japanese killed and 43 taken prisoner, with just 7 of the Defence Force killed in action (Horton 1970, 246).

Coastwatchers

At least as important as the formal military units raised by the warring powers were the thousands of islanders who contributed as "coastwatchers." Most of these worked with Allied networks—either in rear areas such as Vanuatu or New Caledonia, or behind Japanese lines in Papua New Guinea and the Solomon Islands. Small groups of island recruits supported Allied officers with radios in transmitting valuable information back to military command centers. Many islanders proved themselves to be extremely adept in the arts of deception and intelligence gathering. There are numerous independent examples from Papua New Guinea and the Solomon Islands of men who gained access to Japanese camps by offering to sell food or provide labor. Well-educated men with previous government service would present themselves as primitive "natives" by appearing disheveled, dressing up only in a loincloth, and feigning ignorance of English. In the case of the Guadalcanal campaign, the first Allied offensive in the Pacific, information supplied by coastwatchers proved to be critical, as officers hidden in Japanese-held islands north of Guadalcanal radioed advance notice of enemy planes and ships moving southward. In the words of Adm. William Halsey, commander of Allied forces in the South Pacific, "The coastwatchers saved Guadalcanal, and Guadalcanal saved the Pacific." To this we should add, "and the islanders saved the coastwatchers."

Although Halsey was probably referring to the small number of Europeans who remained "in the bush" for coastwatching, in fact "the coastwatchers" included not only the scouts and former police who served with them, but also countless islanders who formed an invisible network of surveillance and assistance. Villagers and local scouts rescued hundreds of pilots downed in remote areas. Some islanders rescued Allied flyers, some rescued Japanese, and many assisted both sides out of a basic sympathy for human suffering. More Allied planes were lost over Papua New Guinea than any other single campaign of any war. In the Solomon Islands alone, it is estimated that about 188 Allied airmen were returned by coastwatching networks (Lord 1977, 293). There were also instances in which the survivors of sunken ships, such as the famous *PT-109* rammed in the Western Solomons, owed their lives to alert scouts and villagers.

Islanders often risked their own lives to rescue servicemen, using great ingenuity to return them safely. In one incident, Guadalcanal villagers hid an

New Georgia, Solomon Islands, 1943.
New Georgia men (Ishmael Ngatu, left; Bill Bennett, center) with a captured Japanese pilot. The coastwatching unit in New Georgia took more than twenty prisoners over the course of a year of intense activity between 1942 and 1943.
(*Source:* Australian War Memorial.)

Noumea, New Caledonia, November 1942.
Local coastwatchers on guard at their post overlooking Noumea harbor receive a visit from a "liberty party" of sailors from the USS *Enterprise.*
(*Source:* National Archives, U.S. Navy.)

Marakei, Kiribati (Gilbert Islands), July 1944.
Islanders rescue a U.S. Navy pilot after he made an emergency landing with his seaplane in their lagoon.
(*Source:* National Archives, U.S. Navy.)

American flyer and attempted to return him by canoe:

> They hadn't gone far when a Jap patrol boat spotted them. The natives quickly pushed the flyer overboard, gave him a long hollow reed [to breathe], then pushed him under the canoe. A few seconds later the patrol boat reached them and the natives were looking at searchlights and machine guns and answering questions. Finally they convinced the Japs that they were night fishing (Budd 1989, 19).

Although established as a passive intelligence-gathering network, some coastwatchers engaged in guerrilla actions that were highly effective in harassing and confusing much larger Japanese forces. One of the most well known of these groups was that headed by Donald Kennedy—a government district officer prior to the war who took up a coastwatching post in New Georgia during the critical years of Japanese occupation in 1942 and 1943. Beginning with a small band of five Solomon Islands police, a few old rifles, and a radio, Kennedy and his men built a well-organized force of twenty-nine fully armed soldiers and forty carriers—all equipped with Japanese uniforms and weapons. Not only did they provide advance information about Japanese air raids to the U.S. troops on Guadalcanal, they also attacked Japanese patrols on a number of occasions. In several well-publicized exploits, Kennedy's "army" (Boutilier 1989) surprised small groups of Japanese, accounting for nearly eighty killed or taken prisoner while losing none of their own. The skills of the scouts in moving around in the forest and on the sea provided them an important advantage in these confrontations. In one instance recalled by Kennedy's right-hand man, a Solomon Islander named Bill Bennett, a group of scouts relied upon their sense of smell to locate an elusive Japanese radio patrol and wiped it out in a surprise attack (White et al. 1988, 142–43). In one surreptitious nighttime operation, a group of Kennedy's scouts made off with a diesel engine, stolen from under the noses of Japanese guards. Small incidents such as these, combined with the unexplained disappearance of patrols, must have created great anxiety among Japanese garrisons operating in New Georgia and elsewhere in the Solomons.

While Kennedy and his coastwatchers lost no men in their engagements, others situated to the north of them in Papua New Guinea were not so lucky. On New Ireland, near the Japanese stronghold at Rabaul, thirty-six coastwatchers, European and Melanesian, lost their lives during the occupation (Murray 1967, 239). One of these was a respected New Ireland elder, Boski, who, after risking his life repeatedly to assist coastwatchers operating in that island, was betrayed by local rivals and beheaded by the Japanese in a public ceremony.

In some cases, small patrols of Papua New Guinea men functioned as guerrilla units (e.g., Ryan 1960). The risks of working behind Japanese lines were tremendous, as illustrated by the experience of twelve men (including five New Guineans) who landed by submarine at Hollandia to reconnoiter Japanese positions prior to the Allied invasion. Three were killed the first day, and only seven survived, wounded and emaciated, after dispersing into the bush without food or supplies (Feldt 1946, 225–33). One of the Papua New Guineans on this mission, Yali Singina, escaped by making an epic three-month trek through 120 miles of jungle back to Allied lines at Aitape. This journey and other wartime experiences contributed to Yali's reputation, and he emerged as the leader of one of the largest political (cargo) movements in postwar Papua New Guinea (Lawrence 1964).

Heroes and Medals

As is usual in war, those who distinguished themselves in combat were honored with medals for bravery. Among the 120 Fijians participating in the recapture of New Georgia, eleven were killed and twenty wounded. Medals received by Fijians throughout the Solomons campaign include one posthumous Victoria Cross, two military crosses, four Distinguished Conduct Medals, sixteen Military Medals, and two U.S. Silver Stars (Ravuvu 1974, 57). A sampling of awards for Papua New Guineans decorated for bravery turns up a number of remarkable cases. For example, the citation for Sgt. William Matpi of Manus Island concludes by noting that he was officially credited with personally killing 110 of the enemy (Barrett 1969, 494)!

In some instances, the heroic exploits of certain individuals, such as the late Sir Jacob Vouza of Guadalcanal (Lord 1977, 57–60) or Sergeant Yauwika of Bougainville, were singled out for prominent attention by the Allied military and media (e.g., Cooper 1946). But for each Vouza there were scores of others whose stories are known only to the men they fought with, and the villages to which they returned.

New Georgia, Solomon Islands, July 1943.
(l. to r.): Pvt. Simate Mahe, Pvt. John Vave, Sgt. John Inu. Three Tongan "warriors" upon return from patrol near Munda in which Vave was wounded three times and Inu rescued a wounded American.
(*Source:* National Archives, U.S. Army Signal Corps.)

Guadalcanal, Solomon Islands, September 1943. Sgt. Maj. Jacob Vouza points to his bar of four medals, including the American Silver Star and the British King George medal, with Maj. Leland Chapman (USMC). After he bravely resisted Japanese attempts at interrogation and was bayoneted and left for dead, Vouza managed to crawl to the U.S. Marine position on Guadalcanal and give them valuable information. For this he was made an honorary sergeant major in the Marine Corps and decorated repeatedly by American and British forces.
(*Source:* National Archives, U.S. Marine Corps.)

Unknown Soldiers

An example of an islander who performed remarkable feats but has not received a place in written history is George Maelalo of Malaita, Solomon Islands (White et al. 1988). Maelalo was recruited (without knowing what he was getting into) by a British district officer, issued a uniform and rifle, and sent to a camp down the coast for training. Within two months his training was cut short because of the urgent need for scouts on Guadalcanal. Beginning with the arduous Guadalcanal campaign, Maelalo and twenty-two other Solomon Islanders fought under the command of British officers through the entire Solomons campaign—from Guadalcanal through New Georgia to Bougainville. Of the twenty-three men who began this odyssey, only seven survived. Despite the fact that these men saw regular front-line action for nearly two years, none received medals or other forms of recognition. Maelalo and fellow Solomon Islanders in his unit are pictured in a British wartime booklet but mistakenly captioned as Fijians (Cooper 1946, 54).

In addition to those who actually took up arms in support of either the Allied or Japanese cause, there were thousands who provided military or humanitarian aid to the combatants without being members of formal military units. Most instances of native attacks against the Japanese will never be recognized because they are recorded only in oral tradition. The unpublished diary of a Catholic priest, Fr. Emery de Klerk, on Guadalcanal indicates something of the extent of those unrecorded actions. Over a two-month pe-

riod in 1942 during the Guadalcanal campaign, Fr. de Klerk noted the following incidents in his diary: "The villagers had killed sixteen Japs three days
before . . . The Japs were caught destroying native gardens which angered the
natives. They surrounded the Japs in the Lunga River and killed them with
spears and axes" (September 11). "Received news that seven natives have
killed the nine Japanese radio crew at Cape Hunter and destroyed the wire-
less station" (October 27). "Forty Nala bush guards arrived armed with Jap
rifles to report for further orders after killing fifty-three Japs" (October 31).

Maprik, Papua New Guinea, 1945. A New Guinean wounded by machine-gun fire while on sentry duty is carried to safety and watched over by Australian soldiers. (*Source:* Australian War Memorial.)

4. Suffering

All the clans . . . who were once brave, courageous, and strong seemed to become like babies in their first day out of their mother's womb. The landing of the Japanese, gun noises, and the actual sight of the ships seemed to have removed the bones of the people. They could not run and even if they did try to run, they could not. It was a unique disaster beyond anybody's memory. . . .

That afternoon . . . there was no time to go to your village to gather your family or collect your valuable belongings. Wife ran naked without her husband and children. Husband ran naked without his wife and children. A child ran without his parents . . . All ran in different directions into the bush. All ran like rats and bandicoots in the Kunai grass. The night fell and each individual slept either in the grass or under trees. The soil was your bed and the rotten logs your pillow. You go to sleep wherever you happened to run to. The noise of the guns died down at night.

The words above are those of Arthur Duna of the village of Konje, describing the Japanese landings near Buna on the north coast of Papua New Guinea (Waiko 1988, 46). Duna and his fellow villagers had the misfortune to be living near the beach where the Japanese made their first landing on the Papua New Guinea mainland. They became caught up in the epic struggle that ensued as Allied forces attempted to retake the area. Duna's words, often poetic, capture the sense of amazement, shock, and intense fear that gripped many islanders who found themselves in the path of the warring forces. For most islanders living in or near combat zones, his words ring true: "It was a unique disaster beyond anybody's memory."

Above: **Kakambona, Guadalcanal, Solomon Islands,
January 25, 1943.
Shell craters and foxholes dot
Kakambona Beach—evidence
of the U.S. bombardment the
day before that drove Japanese from the area. A
Solomon Islands laborer
looks on as the shore is
turned into a supply dump
and bivouac area for the
First Battalion, 27th Infantry.**
(*Source:* National Archives,
U.S. Army Signal Corps.)

The hundreds of islands and atolls stretching across the Pacific Ocean were affected in many different ways by the war. In parts of the Papua New Guinea highlands, large populations remained unaware that a war was taking place, even as coastal areas were in the throes of European evacuation and Japanese occupation. In "staging" areas outside of the war zones, many islanders enjoyed the added excitement and even profited from their interactions with the new outsiders. But in those islands that became battlegrounds, every form of disruption and degradation occurred, ranging from the inconvenience of severed communications to the devastation of entire communities.

Daily life on many islands became harsh and regimented as islanders were recruited to work for victory—Micronesians for the Japanese, Polynesians for the Allies, and Melanesians for both sides. The labor needs of both sides were a major source of disruption for island communities, with extraordinary numbers of young men being recruited and taken away from home (see chapter 5). In some cases recruitment decimated whole villages, and even islands, removing those capable of work for extended periods of time. In one of the more extreme examples, more than half of the people of Nauru (800 out of 1,700) were taken by the Japanese to work at Truk, over a thousand miles to the northwest.

As battles raged, areas occupied by the Japanese were cut off from supply lines, bombed incessantly and, in some cases, invaded with massive force. As Japanese troops became increasingly desperate, their relations with islanders deteriorated badly, often leading to further suffering and death. In the case of the Nauruans on Truk, which was "isolated" and neutralized by American strategy, 473 of the 800 people taken there to work died before the end of the war. The death toll of islanders killed by the warring powers, either accidentally or deliberately, will never be known. It is estimated that in Papua New Guinea alone 15,000 villagers perished in the fighting, bombings, and executions (Oliver 1961, 376).

If separated from sources of supply, servicemen of both sides were taught to live "off the land." In actuality, this usually meant off people's gardens and domestic animals. In the case of the tens of thousands of Japanese in New Guinea cut off from their supply lines for months, desperation led to the exploitation of native communities and to numerous atrocities. One of perhaps the most ignominious fates suffered by islanders during the war was that of the Arapesh individuals who were killed and eaten by starving members of the Japanese 18th Army in 1945 (Tuzin 1983). In many of the Japanese strongholds in Micronesia, where large garrisons were cut off for months by the American advance, islanders suffered starvation alongside the Japanese. Pohnpeian laborers taken to the island of Kosrae recall that as times got tough they were given only swamp taro to eat. But they were better off than the Kiribati (Gilbert Islands) laborers who, as former British subjects, were allowed to eat only small potatoes they could grow (and, in the end, only potato leaves). Many died of malnutrition (Falgout 1989).

Not all the wartime violence came from outside. In some areas, the war intensified traditional rivalries and precipitated renewed fighting. People

Opposite: **Kwajalein, Marshall Islands, February 1, 1944.**
United States troops lead Kwajalein people along the beach for evacuation to nearby Enilapkan Island. The Americans had "run them out of" pillboxes where they had taken refuge during the invasion bombardment. The shoreline of their atoll shows the devastation wrought by the bombardment.
(*Source:* National Archives, U.S. Army Signal Corps.)

found themselves caught up in *two* wars: the global conflict and local struggles. The hasty withdrawal of colonial authorities created widespread fears that warfare would once again break out between traditional enemies. For example, the people of Vanatinai (then Sudest Island), who had once lived in fear of attack by fierce raiders from neighboring islands, promptly evacuated their coastal villages when the government disappeared. At the Iatmul village of Timbunke, ninety-six men and one woman suspected of collaboration with the Australians were massacred by natives from other Sepik villages acting under Japanese orders (Gewertz 1983, 137).

The question of loyalty posed a difficult and often fatal dilemma for islanders, for many of whom the war was a little-understood conflict between outside forces. Many were captured, imprisoned, and even executed as spies by

Noemfoor, Irian Jaya (Dutch New Guinea), July 1944. Caught in the tides of battle, Papuans who had lived under Japanese occupation for two years are here picked up and transported to Allied positions by the U.S. 158th Infantry. Concerned to display the proper loyalties, the group carries two long flagpoles with the Dutch flag (although the "chief" standing at right still wears a Japanese coat).
(*Source:* National Archives, U.S. Army Signal Corps.)

one side or the other. As the only American territory in Micronesia—invaded by the Japanese on the same day as Pearl Harbor—the people of Guam especially suffered for their pro-American sentiments. Scores of people were executed for sheltering American servicemen or otherwise opposing the Japanese regime (see Palomo 1984).

The reversals suffered by the Japanese in many areas, such as the Solomon Islands and Papua New Guinea, frequently led local populations to take on a more aggressive posture in gathering intelligence and carrying out guerrilla actions. These actions in turn evoked retribution. In Irian Jaya, where cult activity was widespread during the war and many people actively resisted the Japanese, hundreds were killed in executions and punitive massacres. Testimony at the postwar trial of the Japanese commander on New Ireland revealed that forty New Guineans had been executed under his command. And the executions in Papua New Guinea did not stop with Allied victory. With the resumption of their own control, Australian authorities hanged ten Papuans for treason (Nelson 1980b, 253).

Uprooting and Evacuation

For people who find their identity and well-being rooted in the land, forced movement away from villages and ancestral lands was one of the most bitter experiences of the war. As Japanese forces advanced southward, many villagers living along the coasts abandoned their settlements and took refuge in rugged inland regions. New Guineans such as Arthur Duna who were forced to move inland became weak and vulnerable refugees. One recalls being

Bougainville, Papua New Guinea, October 1945. Taking what few belongings they are able to carry, residents of Bougainville who had been evacuated by the Japanese to Fauro Island board a barge to return to the Buin area for "rehabilitation" under the supervision of ANGAU (Australian New Guinea Administrative Unit) authorities.
(*Source:* Australian War Memorial.)

questioned by inland residents: "Who are you? Are you beggars? Are you birds from the sea that have no place to land?" Peter Beck of New Georgia, occupied for over a year by Japanese forces, remembers, "The flight of the people sometimes took place in torrential rain, or cold . . . The hunger was terrible and in some places one taro sufficed for five or six people's appetites. The children often cried and nursing mothers wept because they were suckling babies."

For people accustomed to living in villages along the sea, hiding in forest refuges or camping out at garden sites was highly stressful. Memories of these experiences recall a period fraught with danger and uncertainty. Customary activities such as bathing and washing clothes in the sea had to be abandoned. Residents of the coast of Santa Isabel bordering the straights known as "The Slot," where Japanese convoys ran back and forth to Guadalcanal, remember that oil and debris from sunken ships and planes made the sea unusable for ordinary purposes such as making salt. Gardening was especially difficult because fires could not be lit for fear of attracting bombing or strafing attacks. In addition to the physical discomfort of living in temporary shelters, the evacuation threatened people's very sense of community, reversing some of the basic principles of cultured life. Those islanders formerly living in peace along the coast found themselves scattered in interior regions, eating raw foods, unable to worship in church, and living in fear of the destructive effects of war—either from the invaders or from a resurgence of traditional fighting.

Guadalcanal, Solomon Islands, December 1942. Eight Catholic sisters evacuated from Malaita Island arrive on Guadalcanal. Following the Japanese execution of missionaries on Guadalcanal and elsewhere, U.S. commanders ordered the evacuation of all mission stations in the area. The sisters, from the island of Malaita are (l. to r.): unidentified, Aloasia, Bernadetta, unidentified, unidentified, unindentified, Sesarina, and Modesta Oniasi.
(*Source:* National Archives, U.S. Marine Corps.)

In other areas, villagers were evicted from their settlements as military authorities on both sides moved people out of the way to construct bases. The Americans cleared people off Mavea in Vanuatu to use the island for recreation and target practice. Nearly the entire population of Nissan (Green) Island was evacuated by the American forces to Guadalcanal, where many died of malaria before being returned. At Ulithi, site of a large Allied naval base, islanders were concentrated on a few of the atoll's islets. On those islets that were evacuated, people's houses were bulldozed and much of the surface paved to make way for military construction. On Guam, the American bombardment to retake the island left nearly 90 percent of the Chamorro population (of twenty-two thousand) homeless. The Chamorros then saw their island turned into an armed camp as U.S. troops, numbering ten times the indigenous population, prepared for their drive on Iwo Jima. On Rennell, where Americans cut down a coconut grove to make room for an airstrip that was never used, the owner, Tekiuniu, composed a song in retaliation:

> Dig up my coconuts, remove my house
> kill my forest trees
> as the *gemeji* of harvest songs.
>
> Would there were a path to tread upon,
> as I would retaliate, such my thought
> as I ravage America I lay waste.

Separation

The massive and often chaotic movement of people during the war—for refuge, for labor, and for fighting—separated mothers and sons, husbands and wives, and kin from kin for months and even years at a time with no certainty that they would ever see each other again. The intensive recruiting of workers and soldiers left many communities empty of young men and struggling to survive. It was up to the women and children at home, who are often left out of war histories, to sustain communities bereft of young men. The following song composed by Gavide, an old woman of Kotaure in Papua New Guinea, reflects the sadness and bitterness experienced by many women who watched their loved ones depart to help the foreigners with their war (Waiko 1986, 31):

> War has come.
> The young men are leaving
> to defend alien land.
> The foreigners will be saved.
>
> What has called
> the young men away
> to become enemy victims?
> The conquerors will be happy.

The mother is deserted
lonely without her son
a barren beggar
abandoned to heartache.

The mother who lost blood
has become a barren beggar.
The one who bore him
I am a lonely beggar.

Bombing

Islanders remember attempts by both the Japanese and Allied forces to keep them out of targeted areas, but hundreds if not thousands nonetheless fell victim to bombing raids. In addition to soldiers and scouts on the front lines, carriers, laborers, and ordinary villagers were frequently subjected to deadly bombings. On January 4, 1942, initiating their invasion of Rabaul, Japanese bombs killed twelve islanders and wounded thirty who were caught in the open on a golf links. Shortly after the first recruits of the Solomon Islands Labour Corps assembled for work on Guadalcanal, their camp was bombarded by Japanese planes leaving eleven dead and nine wounded. The men refused to work until cajoled back on the job by British authorities. Somu Sigob, a member of the Papua New Guinea police during the war, recalls the similar plight of New Guinea carriers: "At one stage the Australian soldiers fired mortars, but they miscalculated . . . when the mortars exploded close to us, the labourers ran for their lives . . . they didn't head for Port Moresby but ran through the bush until they reached their villages. Later the *kiaps* [government officers] caught them, gave them some punishments and then sent them back" (Sigob 1975, 32).

Innocent villagers were often the victims of indiscriminate bombing. As John B. Lundstrom, historian of the naval air war, has commented, "In reading the reports, I get the impression that little thought was given to warning the pilots of the presence of friendly natives. They had leave to attack everything they thought might be military objectives without determining whether the Japanese were actually present" (letter to Hugh Laracy, Sept. 12, 1988).

The action report for one flight of seven torpedo planes described a bombing run as follows:

An approach up to the western coast of Malaita was then made in an effort to reach Coleridge Bay and bomb Japanese forces located there. Langa-Langa Harbor was mistaken for Coleridge Bay . . . Several large clusters of native huts were observed. Seaplane and motorboat moorings were observed. An attack was made with bombs on the largest of these clusters, setting it afire.

In this case, however, there were no Japanese—only islanders, residents of the settlement known as Laulasi built on an artificial island in the Langa-

Nissan (Green) Island, Papua
New Guinea, February 1944.
Some of the 1,000 residents of
Nissan Island who were removed from their home to
make room for the construction of a U.S. base are here
shown boarding the landing
ship that transported them
hundreds of miles to the
south to Guadalcanal where
they remained under Allied
care for seven months.
(*Source:* National Archives,
U.S. Marine Corps.)

Aola, Guadalcanal, Solomon Islands, February 1944.
Nissan (Green) Islanders disembark with their possessions from the landing ships that transported them to their destination. The evacuation, which had been ordered by ANGAU, proved to be very costly for the Nissan Islanders, as 148 died in the ensuing months, and many were reported to be "psychologically dispirited." (*Source:* National Archives, U.S. Army Signal Corps.)

Falalop, Ulithi, Federated States of Micronesia, October 1944.
A Seabee bulldozer tears down a large house in a village to make way for a Marine camp on Falalop Island in Ulithi, Caroline Islands. (*Source:* National Archives, U.S. Navy.)

Langa lagoon. The one-hundred-pound bombs and incendiary clusters dropped on Laulasi killed at least eighteen of them, mostly children. As one of the residents of Laulasi recalled years later,

The whole village was on fire. At that time everybody was wondering where to take cover or shelter so some people were killed by the bombs, some were very old people and they could not run quickly from the fire. At that moment fathers and mothers could not do anything more to help their families. They had to save their own lives. People just ran naked and swam to the nearest islands, to the reefs and to the mainland. Some went in their canoes . . . At that time they were just clothed with torn bags (Keeble 1980, 7).

The British Resident Commissioner, who had taken refuge in the Malaita hills only a short distance away, wrote in his diary that day, "7 U.S. planes bombed Laulasi village—18 killed—most inexplicable as no enemy reported there."

Although the Laulasi bombing was one of the more destructive, numerous other indiscriminate bombings created real problems for Allied efforts to retain the loyalty of islanders. On the island of Santa Isabel, the very Defence Force scouts who were supplying Allied pilots with intelligence information watched their own village bombed. They immediately threatened to cease their intelligence gathering unless guarantees could be given against further incidents.

Other people died in deliberate bombing raids carried out by both sides against those villages suspected of collaboration. Admiral Halsey recalled,

Saipan, Northern Mariana Islands, June 1944. Residents of Saipan, who had been "ferreted out of the hills" by U.S. Marines, board a truck that will transport them to a rear area. The 4,000 or so Chamorro and Carolinian Islanders who had lived in Saipan for thirty years under Japanese rule were initially under suspicion and placed in detention camps. (*Source:* National Archives, U.S. Marine Corps.)

Guam, n.d.
**Women wash clothes in a
shell crater at one of the
camps set up to house the
thousands of people left
without homes following the
Japanese occupation and U.S.
invasion.**
(*Source:* National Archives,
U.S. Marine Corps.)

Guam, August 1944.
A Chamorro woman suffering
from malnutrition is carried
in from the hills where she
and her family had been hid-
ing during the Japanese
occupation. Following the
U.S. counterinvasion, in
which scores of Guamanian
people died, hundreds who
had remained loyal to the
United States came out of the
hills to receive food and hos-
pital care.
(*Source:* National Archives,
U.S. Marine Corps.)

"Most of the natives were loyal to the Allies, but the Japs occasionally managed to corrupt a village. As soon as we heard of it, we would bomb the village, then drop pidgin English messages on the villages near by, warning them not to invite bombs on themselves" (Halsey and Bryan 1947, 150). A copy of one such message dropped on Bougainville in January 1943 reads as follows (in English translation):

A serious warning from the big white chief to all natives of Buka Passage, Buin, and Kieta: . . . The village of Sorum has been disloyal, has taken orders from the Japs, and has helped the Japs. We have now bombed them. We also bombed Pidia, Pok Pok, Toberoi, and Sadi when they helped the Japs. If any villages help the Japs we will bomb them and destroy them altogether. We have many planes, many bombs and many soldiers. We will not hesitate to carry out this work.

Death

Perhaps the most absolute devastation was experienced by inhabitants of those areas occupied by the Japanese and retaken by American amphibious assault. In Guam, where Chamorro residents had lived for two and a half years under harsh Japanese supervision, numerous atrocities occurred prior to the American invasion in 1944 (e.g., Palomo 1984). Other parts of Micronesia also suffered the full brunt of American assaults. The people of Meden Islet in Enewetak Lagoon have not forgotten the nightmare they experienced at the hands of one apparently brutal Marine officer. On February 4, 1944, the people of Enewetak took cover in bunkers trying to escape an awesome naval

Sipilangan, New Britain, Papua New Guinea, July 1945. Two New Guinean children near death from malnutrition and tropical ulcers receive treatment at an ANGAU refugee camp at Sipilangan. This camp housed about six hundred people who had fled their homes in areas of the island occupied by Japanese forces. Many died from disease and malnutrition while attempting to survive in rugged mountain areas. (*Source:* Australian War Memorial.)

and air barrage (Carucci 1989). Whereas most of the native inhabitants of the lagoon recall being treated well by the American invaders who fought their way ashore, the people of Meden were the victims of a senseless attack. One of the survivors recalls,

From the beginning, those of us on Meden were unfortunate. To begin with there were ships, lagoon and ocean side, and planes helping from above . . . If you wanted to get away, you had to dig, for there was no other place open for escape. From dawn to dusk they shot at this islet. At the finish, there was not a single coconut standing . . . All of us were in the holes. Anything not in the holes disappeared. But even in the shelters there was damage. [Some] died in those holes, some from fragments, but almost all after the soldiers landed.

In the holes it was awful. We were hungry and thirsty, but no one could go out. If you traveled outside you would disappear. So the hole was also bad because we had to pee and shit inside, even desecrate the face of close kin. Then in their coming the [U.S.] warriors were not straight in their work. They came to the shelter of ours, guns ready, and looked toward us inside. So great was our fear that we were all in a corner, like kittens. And then they yelled and threw in a hand grenade.

The soldiers called out to the leaders, "Kanaka, kanaka!" and waited until they responded, and then threw in the hand grenade . . . When it burst, the whole shelter was torn apart. So powerful was the thing one could never stand. Earth fragments struck us, but the others in the other half, they died. All the force of the explosion went over there. . . .

Afterward, we did not move, but stayed there for awhile amidst the dirt and sand, and then they returned to check, and they took us out and stripped us with the bayonets on the fronts of their guns, like some sort of game, and then they took all of us to the field and lined us up and prepared to shoot us. We trembled, so great was our fear, but still they pointed guns at our heads. And then they tied cloth around our heads so you could no longer see in front of you and readied us to be slaughtered. Perhaps some did not wish to, but he [the commanding officer] made them raise their rifles. They quibbled . . . they talked back and he [commander] became enraged . . . We waited. And afterward they took the blindfolds and took us to the ship.

The war's terrors were magnified for people who had lived all their lives in small island communities. Islanders witnessed their atolls, beaches, and land turned into a killing ground. Like Meden Islanders, many communities continue to recall war tragedies in annual performances of war histories, songs, and prayers of thanksgiving. The fighting not only took away loved ones, it permanently marked people and places with the scars of war. These scars, still abundant in the landscape, serve as reminders of the vulnerability of small island communities to the destruction that can be wrought by distant and alien military powers.

Dumpu, Papua New Guinea, January 1944.
With their thumbprints, islanders sign on to work for ANGAU's labor corps. Each wears a numbered dogtag for identification.
(*Source:* Australian War Memorial.)

Kirakira, Makira (San Cristobal), Solomon Islands, June 1943.
New recruits for the Solomon Islands Labour Corps line up for inspection prior to embarking for Guadalcanal. British officers borrowed pre-war plantation methods to organize and oversee workers.
(*Source:* National Archives, U.S. Navy.)

5. Working

Wars are hard work. Pushing into the Pacific islands, the Japanese and the Allied war efforts demanded tremendous amounts of manpower. Both sides established numerous strategic and supply bases dotted throughout the Pacific, and both quickly realized the value of Pacific island labor pools. If combat-trained soldiers might be relieved of everyday military "housekeeping" duties, then these men could be shifted forward to the battle lines. War bases were labor magnets. They pulled thousands of Pacific islanders out of backwater lagoon villages and isolated mountain hamlets—many from islands hundreds of miles distant from the site of a base itself.

As pictured in preceding sections, a significant number of islanders went to war and fought under the command of the Allies or Japanese. Others suffered the war, victims of bombings and population displacement. Most people's war experiences, however, were predominantly working encounters. Those islanders who undertook the day-to-day tasks of unloading ships, carrying supplies, stretcher-bearing, cultivating crops, constructing roads, airfields and buildings, mosquito abatement, laundry, janitorial, and garbage details, among others, kept turning the small but essential wheels of war.

Someone had to unload, move about, and reload the tons of cargo that made battles possible. The U.S. military employed 1,500 New Caledonians out of an approximate indigenous population of 30,000. Positioning themselves to attack Japanese positions to the north, the Americans next moved into Vanuatu and employed more than 1,000 local people on Efate Island and over 500 on Espiritu Santo. In Fiji, 1,375 men had joined the First Battalion, Fiji Labour Corps by the end of 1942. A company of these men subsequently embarked for Bougainville to work as stevedores at the new American base at Torokina.

In the Solomon Islands, 3,200 men worked on Guadalcanal, the Russells,

Kirakira, Makira (San Cristobal), Solomon Islands, June 1943.
Maj. C. V. Widdy, chief manager for Levers Pacific Plantations before the war, gives a potential labor corps recruit a cursory medical examination.
(*Source:* National Archives, U.S. Navy.)

Guadalcanal, Solomon Islands, September 1943.
Workers in the Solomon Islands Labour Corps were paid one shilling (sixteen cents) a day, but often received far more in food, clothing, and equipment given away by American troops. Many workers had a trade box, such as that shown here, to carry the booty back home to their villages. In some instances, colonial officials confiscated these acquisitions, creating lasting resentments.
(*Source:* National Archives, U.S. Marine Corps.)

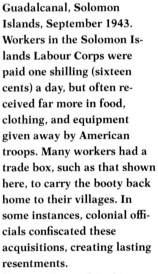

**Ilolo, Papua New Guinea,
March 1944.**
**Workers from the Ilolo area
near Port Moresby line up for
an ANGAU roll call parade in
the early morning mist, before going to work in a
logging area.**
(*Source:* Australian War
Memorial.)

and at Tulagi. Those on Guadalcanal were joined by 400 Gilbert Islanders working alongside. Monthly labor strengths in Papua New Guinea peaked at nearly 38,000 men in June of 1944 (compared with an estimated total of 50,000 in the prewar plantation labor force [Nelson 1980b, 248]). This figure does not count those working for the Japanese, nor an unknown number of laborers working for the Americans as well as for the Japanese in what was then Dutch New Guinea. As late as January 1945—after the action of battle had shifted far to the north—1,487 men still labored for the Americans in Samoa, 229 in Fiji, and 137 in Funafuti, the capital of Tuvalu. In addition to labor corps recruits, large numbers of other islanders worked for the military as casual or day-laborers.

In some islands and villages, virtually every able-bodied man joined military labor corps. Attempts were sometimes made to limit the social effects of recruitment on village life; Australian New Guinea Administrative Unit (ANGAU) officers were initially ordered not to recruit more than 25 percent of the local male population (Robinson 1981, 15). As fighting grew fierce and military needs expanded, however, this limit was ignored and recruitment levels often reached 100 percent. Every man, beginning with fourteen-year-old boys, had gone to war.

In Vanuatu, nearly 1,000 men from Tanna Island went north to Efate to work at the American advanced base code-named "Roses." The total population of the island at the time was not much more than 6,000. A Tannese string band, in a song still popular today, sings about wartime labor migration in Vanuatu pidgin English:

> Taem U.S. i kasem Efate, big fraet i kam antap;
> nao i stat blong tekem ol man i helpem hem;
> sendem tok i kam long saoten aelan;
> Tanna i saplae 1,000 pipol i go wok long Port Vila.
>
> (When the U.S. reached Efate, there was much fear;
> then they began recruiting everyone to help;
> sent a message to the southern islands;
> Tanna supplied 1,000 people who went to work at Port Vila.)

How were these thousands of Pacific islanders recruited? In Japanese-occupied territory, such as around Rabaul, New Britain, the military ordered village chiefs to provide in rotation manpower for military labor needs—including road construction, cargo carrying, firewood collection, and the like.

Behind Allied lines, the U.S. Army and Navy generally worked with existing colonial governments when hiring local manpower. Colonial agents went into local villages, lined up men and boys, gave them a cursory health examination, and signed up recruits they delivered to the bases.

In Papua New Guinea, ANGAU organized the recruitment and supervision of native labor. In the Solomon Islands, the remnant British colonial administration established the Solomon Island Labour Corps (SILC) in November

Guam, August 1944.
Chamorros line up at the Marine Corps Civil Affairs hut for work assignments, after the liberation of their island.
(*Source:* National Archives, U.S. Marine Corps.)

Noumea, New Caledonia, February 1943.
The day shift of the Port Company forms up on the Grand Quay docks. Islanders in labor corps found their lives organized according to various military practices, such as the formation seen here. Like Noumea, many Pacific ports operated both day and night.
(*Source:* National Archives, U.S. Army Signal Corps.)

Noumea, New Caledonia, November 1942.
New Caledonian dock workers have spaghetti for lunch at their camp outside Noumea, named "Joe Louis" after the black American boxer. The Army's release on this photo notes, "Quartered in U.S. tents, fed and clothed by the U.S., these natives are enjoying 'luxuries' which they never had before."
(*Source:* National Archives, U.S. Army Signal Corps.)

Guadalcanal, Solomon Islands, n.d.
Young Solomon Islands workers eating rice and corn. Although food was plentiful at many bases, it was sometimes nutritionally deficient. Many labor corps members came down with cases of beriberi and dysentery.
(*Source:* Fiji Ministry of Information.)

1942, staffed with British officers who recruited and commanded native labor units "lent" to the U.S. military. The Americans, of course, provided worker and officer salaries, supplies, medical care, and logistical support; the Navy, for example, often furnished ships to transport workers from island to island.

The U.S. military was sometimes displeased with the methods and performance of colonial labor agents. In New Caledonia and Vanuatu, for example, it stepped in and assumed the tasks of labor recruitment and supervision. Here, islanders worked directly for occupying American forces.

In much of the Pacific, islanders were willing recruits. Although military work was often difficult, tedious, and dangerous, bases were nonetheless places of huge excitement. Workers encountered fascinating strangers and astonishing sights unknown before the war. However, in those places where colonial authorities organized native labor corps (such as Micronesia, Samoa, and much of Papua New Guinea), military work was not as novel or attractive. ANGAU in Papua New Guinea, for example, had to dragoon a part of its labor force. Its police went into local villages to conscript workers. ANGAU also faced a desertion problem as unwilling workers attempted to escape to their homes (Robinson 1981, 66–78).

In places where workers were poorly treated, islanders were also slow to recruit. Exworkers report one stratagem resorted to in response to labor shortages on New Britain: The Japanese invited people to feasts and then impressed all those who attended into their military labor gangs.

Allied labor recruiting was more regularized. Workers in Vanuatu, for example, signed on for three-month tours of duty. In New Caledonia, tours of

Guadalcanal, Solomon Islands, January 1943. Workers line up to receive weekly wages of five shillings (eighty cents) from an Australian supervisor. Although the American military provided the funds for labor corps operations, the prewar colonial powers demanded to control wage payments to island workers, hoping to contain the American influence. Note the military cameraman at work. (*Source:* National Archives, U.S. Marine Corps.)

duty were increased to four months due to a shrinking labor pool. In the Solomons and Papua New Guinea, where the press of battle was much greater, labor contracts typically ran for six months, a year, or longer. Some workers in New Guinea served two years or more. Micronesians similarly worked steadily throughout the war right up until the time their islands were surrendered by the Japanese.

Conditions of work and supervision of labor varied from base to base, depending on whether Americans, Australians, British, or Japanese were in command and on the progression of the war itself. Generally, however, workers were organized into work teams of twenty to twenty-five men, one or two of whom were appointed "sergeants" or, in the old plantation jargon, "boss-boys"—their promotion based often on their knowledge of some English, pidgin English, or Japanese.

New recruits received clothing, some token of identification, and a few personal supplies, along with a cot in a military canvas tent. In New Caledonia this amounted to two blankets, two uniforms, a jacket, shoes, and a dogtag. The Japanese in New Britain provided workers with identity cards, with small pieces of wood marked with a man's name, number, and village, or with numbered strips of white cloth worn around the arm. In Papua New Guinea, ANGAU commonly provided only cloth lavalavas (or *laplaps*), as prewar colonial policy discouraged islanders from wearing pants or shirts (Ryan 1969).

The tropical day is almost evenly divided between night and day. Military work began early. After a dawn line-up, labor gangs marched off to work. Some teams clambered aboard trucks, often driven by black American servicemen, and rode to the docks. Other teams, on long marches to the battle lines along bush trails, shouldered their loads at sunup. Each man carried

Wanigela, Papua New Guinea, October 1942. Villagers unload equipment of the 2/6th Australian Independent Company during the Allied advance on Buna. Casual workers such as these sometimes received a little tobacco or other goods in payment for their labor. (*Source:* Australian War Memorial.)

Kiriwina, Papua New Guinea, July 1943. Children carry ashore U.S. Army supplies landed on a jetty in the Trobriand Islands.
(*Source:* National Archives, U.S. Army Signal Corps.)

about forty pounds of ammunition, food supplies, water, or military mail sacks. For example, along the Kokoda Trail—which climbs the precipitous Owen Stanley Mountains in Papua New Guinea—carriers who reached the front set down one load and hoisted a second for the return trip. They also picked up the wounded on stretchers and carefully carried these men back down muddy trails to coastal hospitals.

Other island workers, after morning line-up, rode or marched to airfields under construction where they laid down steel (Marsden) matting; to motor pools where they washed jeeps and cleaned used parts; to construction sites where they helped build warehouses, fuel tanks, churches, roads, and bridges; to docks and warehouses where they loaded and unloaded ships and trucks; to military farms where they cultivated corn for the Allies and rice for the Japanese; to laundries and kitchens; and to cemeteries where they tended soldiers' graves. Some laborers stayed in camp to prepare food for their fellow work-team members. Others waited on tables in officers' mess tents. And some worked as scouts, guides, and informants, such as for the *kempeitai*, the Japanese military police.

At the height of the war, islanders frequently worked ten hours a day, sometimes more. In Vanuatu, before and during the Guadalcanal offensive, work-

Guadalcanal, Solomon Islands, March 1943. Members of the Solomon Islands Labour Corps offload gasoline drums along the coast of Guadalcanal. Less than a year earlier, this area was nothing but plantation land. By this time it was one of the busiest ports in the Pacific, as can be seen by the ships in the background. (*Source:* National Archives, U.S. Navy.)

Above: **Nanumea, Tuvalu (Ellice Islands), September 1943. As U.S. forces arrive on Nanumea Island, islanders and Marines transfer water tins from a naval boat to outrigger canoes that can negotiate the shallow waters over the coral reef.**
(*Source:* National Archives, U.S. Marine Corps.)

Left: **Aitape, Papua New Guinea, August 1944. Villagers unload supplies fixed to poles from an amphibious "Duck" for their daily trek to the front lines. On the way back, they evacuate the wounded. Carriers often came under fire.**
(*Source:* National Archives, U.S. Army Signal Corps.)

ers split into shifts and moved cargo day and night, the docks made bright by lights powered by electric generators. These efforts were exacted of both Allied and Japanese labor recruits. More than two days rest a month was uncommon. Isaac Gafu, a Solomon Islands laborer, recalls, "We became so absorbed with the work that we did not know which day was Sunday or which one was Saturday. Every week was just like the one before. Every day was just the same. We had not time to rest. We just worked" (Ngwadili et al. 1988, 207).

As the Allies increased pressure on Japanese positions, labor conditions deteriorated. Pohnpeians and other Micronesians working for the Japanese struggled daily to repair facilities damaged in American bombings and to grow sorely needed crops. In some areas, whole villages were mobilized to support intensive agricultural schemes aimed at provisioning the war effort. For example, the Japanese introduced rice plantations in New Guinea, and manioc (cassava) farms in Palau. By 1944, Palauan production reached three times the assigned quota (1,245 pounds per family per month), exceeding the output of Japanese farmers (Higuchi 1986, 23). In Pohnpei, days off were first reduced to every other Sunday and then canceled altogether. Some workers were locked in their compounds, and other forced to sleep in bunkers that amounted to only crawlspace. A women's song from the manioc fields of wartime Pohnpei tells the story (Falgout 1989, 284):

> Our dwelling makes us really lonely.
> It is worse than being in prison
> because we have assumed the appearance of frogs,
> crawling around and looking straight ahead.

Military necessity often required the recruitment of island women. For example, on one occasion, Fr. Emery de Klerk, a Catholic priest on Guadalcanal, organized sixty women to carry rations for American troops making a foray into the mountains. Each woman carried ten days of rations, amounting to thirty cans, balanced on her head. On neighboring Santa Isabel, where the male population was mostly absent (employed at the American base in the Russell Islands), women worked long hours to produce thatch to be picked up by naval boats and delivered for construction work at the base. The formation of organized women's labor groups, as in parts of Micronesia where labor shortages demanded such measures, was in many instances the first occasion for female participation in the cash economy—a precedent that was not forgotten after the war.

The exchange of goods is an important aspect of personal relationships throughout the Pacific. The way workers remember and evaluate their wartime experiences today is based in large part on the treatment they received from their supervisors—particularly on the quality and quantity of food and other provisions they were given in exchange for their labor. Military personnel who looked after their workers well gained a reputation that in many instances endures today.

Salamaua, Papua New
Guinea, September 1943.
Carriers bear a wounded Australian soldier down a
slippery, muddy trail on Buo-
isi Ridge. Climbing the steep
twenty-five-hundred-foot
ridge took six hours; descend-
ing an hour and a half. It was
this type of work, bearing
stretchers and saving Australian lives, that earned Papua
New Guineans the label
"fuzzy wuzzy angels" in the
popular Australian press.
(*Source:* Australian War
Memorial.

Above: **Ulupu, Papua New Guinea, July 1945.**
Thirty islanders haul a 75mm mountain gun up Ulupu Ridge.
(*Source:* Australian War Memorial.)

Right: **Guadalcanal, Solomon Islands, April 1944.**
An American agricultural expert and two islanders inspect the corn crop at a military farm on Guadalcanal. Islanders worked on military farms on a number of Pacific islands, providing fresh fruit and vegetables for military kitchens and hospitals.
(*Source:* National Archives, U.S. Marine Corps.)

Guam, 1942.
Japanese forces oversee Chamorros working in new rice paddies. Whereas the Americans planted corn, the Japanese grew rice in the areas they occupied, including Papua New Guinea. Both sides pretended that agricultural labor "promoted dietary self-sufficiency and a will to work" among islanders.
(*Source:* Kyuya Takenaka.)

Guadalcanal, Solomon Islands, 1943.
Islanders work with American Seabees, leveling Henderson Field.
(*Source:* Naval Construction Battalion Center.)

Depending on location, some workers dined in military mess tents; some cooked for themselves food the military provided; others survived on combat rations. Carriers who walked seven days through cold mountains from Bulldog to Wau, New Guinea, for example, marched all day on one meal of boiled rice, a few hard biscuits, and some tea and sugar. They were issued small tins of meat when they set out from Bulldog. These they usually ate immediately rather than carry (Ryan 1969, 542). In Vanuatu, conversely, workers recall being unable to eat all the rice, meat, bread, and other provisions they received. Similarly, despite their best efforts, they were unable to smoke every cigarette American servicemen tossed their way.

Gifts of food, cigarettes, and various odd scraps from military warehouses were especially appreciated by workers in light of the low wages they received. Labor corps wages were rarely higher than those paid in prewar plantation economies—and these were abjectly low even for the times. Pacific colonial authorities prevailed upon military employers not to "overpay" native labor lest this induce a postwar wage inflation feared by European planters and other colonial businessmen.

Workers in the Solomon Islands received one pound a month (twenty shillings, or around four dollars). (For sake of comparison, the British officers who commanded the SILC received one pound, two and a half shillings a day.) When a Dutch priest on Guadalcanal advised the Americans to pay native labor *two* shillings a day, he was violently opposed by British officials who insisted on only one. The British did, however, agree that workers would receive a "bonus" of some yardage of cloth, three sticks of tobacco a week, free clay pipes, and the promise of a three-month supply of rice "when available."

Guadalcanal, Solomon Islands, January 1943. American Army Engineers and Solomon Islanders work together, laying Marsden matting at Henderson Field. Work teams composed of *both* islanders and servicemen broke prewar labor patterns.
(*Source:* National Archives, U.S. Army Signal Corps.)

**Espiritu Santo, Vanuatu
(New Hebrides), January 1943.
A Seabee and an island
worker light up together as
they weave coconut leaf
mats, used for house walls
and thatching. The transfer
of technology during the war
was not completely one-way.
The military adopted traditional Pacific architectural
techniques and styles in
many of its temporary con-
structions.**
(*Source:* National Archives,
U.S. Navy.)

Efate, Vanuatu (New Hebrides), February 1944.
A military policeman and George Kalsakau, a member of the British colonial police force, patrol together near Port Vila. Local police served as guides and interpreters for American MPs. The Kalsakau family of Ifira Island remains prominent in Vanuatu today.
(*Source:* National Archives, U.S. Army Signal Corps.)

Tulagi, Nggela (Florida Islands), Solomon Islands, April 1944.
Labor Corps worker tends graves at Navy and Marine Cemetery No. 1. Islanders took care of military graveyards throughout the Pacific. After the war, they also helped disinter the dead when American casualties were repatriated.
(*Source:* National Archives, U.S. Marine Corps.)

In Vanuatu, workers earned one and one-half shillings a day, in Papua New Guinea five to fifteen shillings a month, and in New Caledonia twenty and one-half francs (46 cents) for a fifty-four-hour week. The Japanese paid similarly low wages. At the beginning of the war, islanders on Pohnpei, for example, earned one and one-half yen a day for skilled labor, and one yen for unskilled. Pohnpeian women workers earned less, only three-quarter yen a day (Falgout 1989, 284).

War work was often dangerous. Island workers were sometimes trapped between the two opposing forces when each side bombed or shelled the other's positions. Many workers throughout Micronesia and in Japanese-occupied Papua New Guinea were wounded and killed during American assaults. On Pohnpei, for example, where American strategy called for "neutralizing" rather than invading the island, an estimated 250 bombing strikes were flown against the island between February 1944 and August 1945. They came with such regularity that Pohnpeian laborers working in the fields would time their 8 A.M. breakfast break in their bunkers to coincide with the morning air raid (Falgout 1989). Solomon Island workers were also killed and wounded on several occasions when the Japanese bombed American positions in their archipelago.

Many more workers died of disease (an exact figure is unknown). Medical officers usually were assigned to treat labor corps recruits. Even so, many workers went down with pneumonia, influenza, diarrhea, and beriberi. Some of this illness resulted from a new diet as islanders ate military rations in-

Tuvalu (Ellice Islands), October 1943.
An American sergeant watches as a local girl does his laundry. Laundry was big business at all military bases. Many island women and men made what, to them, were small fortunes; some still have pillow cases full of American half dollars earned washing clothes.
(*Source:* National Archives, U.S. Marine Corps.)

Morobe, Papua New Guinea, July or August 1943. Island mess cook peels potatoes.
(*Source:* National Archives, U.S. Navy.)

stead of traditional Pacific staples. At some U.S. bases, rates of beriberi decreased when doctors diagnosed vitamin deficiencies and ordered unpolished rice for labor corps menus.

Despite low pay, occasional danger, disease, and death, many workers today recall with pleasure their labor corps experiences. The war was an exciting period of unprecedented and unparalleled events. This was a time when some of the most complex products of the industrialized world poured into remote Pacific islands—islands until then mostly ignorant of modern technology. This was also a time to meet strangers and make new friends.

Although the Japanese had colonized Micronesia and America ruled Hawaii, eastern Samoa, and Guam, in many parts of the Pacific these outsiders were unknown. The occupying Japanese and American forces acquired a local social image which, in part, depended on the fact that they were unlike the established colonial powers: the British, Australians, French, and Dutch. Pacific islanders who went to work for the two invading forces soon discovered that relations with military outsiders differed markedly from those they had experienced before the war. Many servicemen shared food, passed around small presents, worked, joked, and danced alongside native labor gangs. Islanders still recall the names of many Americans and Japanese they befriended during the war.

More important, workers also met strangers from within their own countries. The labor corps pulled together people from different islands and different villages. These men, working side by side, had an opportunity to discover and define shared interests and goals. In Papua New Guinea, wartime work fostered the spread of the local pidgin English, Tok Pisin, even more widely than prewar work had done.

Workers sometimes united to protest aspects of military labor itself. In New Caledonia, islanders organized a strike in the early part of the war to protest labor conditions (Oliver 1961, 380). In the Solomon Islands, workers in newfound unity went on strike against low wages or delays in receiving wages. In late 1942, a British labor overseer on Guadalcanal reported, "A group of workers under one Kaparine [were] dismissed after lodging certain most extravagant written demands . . . covering working conditions and payment." Workers continued to protest conditions on Guadalcanal throughout

Morobe(?), Papua New Guinea, June or August 1943. Two young islanders wait on table in a military mess. One serviceman pours out a dose of quinine sulfate.
(*Source:* National Archives, U.S. Navy.)

Yamil, Papua New Guinea, July 1945.
Munhoe and Otalif enjoy a cigarette as they scrub their Australian boss's back, after a day's work in a field hospital laundry.
(*Source:* Australian War Memorial.)

the following year (White et al. 1988, 130–31). Although these actions were mostly unsuccessful in influencing military labor policies, the experience of wartime unity and collective action laid a foundation for the eventual independence of Pacific island nations.

The work of Pacific island laborers facilitated the more deadly tasks of Allied and Japanese servicemen. When island veterans today recollect the war, often what they remember first are their labor corps experiences. In Vanuatu, for example, old labor corps recruits, thinking back to the war, remember the songs they sang while working. These songs celebrate the personal significance of wartime encounters with strangers and new friends. Workers from Tanna, Vanuatu, composed this farewell song for the departing Americans:

> We work for America;
> not knowing when this time will end;
> we wave goodbye to you, United States;
> don't forget about us;
> the things we sing to you;
> goodbye, sometime until we meet again;
> you remember me;
> you United States.

**Guadalcanal, Solomon
Islands, March 1944.**
The amount of supplies
shipped into the Pacific during the war was awesome.
Piles of goods stacked up at
supply dumps gave rise to a
new word in Solomon Islands
pidgin English: *staka*, meaning a "huge amount." Much
of the material was handled
by workers in the Solomon
Islands Labour Corps, shown
here unloading and stacking
cartons of beer.
(*Source:* National Archives,
U.S. Army Signal Corps.)

6. Cargo

The nautical term *cargo* was known throughout the Pacific before World War II. The war, however, universalized the word; battles demand supplies as well as labor. The Japanese and Allied forces both established elaborate transportation networks to bring an incredible variety of goods out to remote Pacific islands. On these islands—at the endpoints of extended military lines of supply—huge amounts of materiel and equipment poured ashore. Pacific islanders witnessed the establishment of supply bases, depots, and dumps. Working alongside port and quartermaster company stevedores, they themselves hefted and stacked much of what needed to be carried ashore. This was the war's cargo, or (in the pidgin English of the Southwest Pacific) "kago."

The amount of military hardware dumped about the Pacific was tremendous. From 1942 to 1945, 4,038,098 measurement tons of cargo left U.S. ports for the Pacific for Army use alone. Another 1,704,389 tons were procured from regional sources, principally Australia and New Zealand (Stauffer 1956, 159). This cargo was stockpiled at bases around the Pacific for local use or for shipment to advanced positions. The small island Saipan in the Marianas, for example, had 1,800,000 square feet of warehouse space built by September 1945 (ibid., 95). Military installations on Guadalcanal covered more than 1,800 acres by the same date. Army quartermasters organized the construction of cities of warehouses near island ports; they also stored caches of cargo at various places in island hinterlands to protect supplies from enemy action. In some cases, as in the Solomon Islands, new national and provincial capitals grew up around the sites of supply bases, with their wartime infrastructures of airfields, warehouses, wharfs, hospitals, and roads.

Both sides imported outside technology into the region in order to get things done. This transfer of technology was not entirely one-way, however. For some tasks, the American military adopted traditional Pacific crafts. Sea-

Banika, Russell Islands, Solomon Islands, January 1945.
On islands where the few existing roads had been built with axes and shovels, mechanized road-building and earth-moving equipment, such as pictured here, made deep impressions. A once placid plantation has become the heavy equipment yard for the largest Marine supply base in the South Pacific.
(*Source:* National Archives, U.S. Marine Corps.)

Pavuvu, Russell Islands, Solomon Islands, August 1944.
Heaps of milk and other Marine food supplies. In traditional exchanges, Pacific islanders also stack up the food they are giving away, but they could not compete with the Marines. Sights such as this were recollected in postwar "cargo" movements.
(*Source:* National Archives, U.S. Marine Corps.)

bees, for example, learned from island teachers how to produce coconut thatching for use at Halavo, Nggela (Florida Islands) and other bases.

War photographs capture something of the magnitude of these military hoards: piles of rations and heaps of beer; fields of planes; yards of heavy equipment; rows of jeeps; the jumble of goods landed on beachheads during every battle. At one point, there were fleets of ships anchored off Manus Island, and a Coca Cola bottling plant working on shore. Songs composed around the Pacific express a fascination and astonishment over new objects observed. A Vanuatu example proclaims:

> Happiness, astonishment here;
> We saw many things:
> airplanes, submarines, tractors, autos.
> The land was too small;
> they were like the sand and the stars in the sky,
> impossible to count

Before the war, most islanders had little contact with the products of metropolitan, industrialized societies. Their contact with the wider world was mostly limited to the comings and goings of inter-island boats that carried labor recruiters, missionaries, colonial officials, and imported only simple manufactured products from the outside world. War technology, on the other hand, was immense, powerful, and often difficult to comprehend. Isaac Gafu of Malaita Island describes the shock of the new: "You would be looking at

Hanuabada Village, Port Moresby, Papua New Guinea, January 1943.
Bulk fuel storage tank being constructed for the Australian military. Islanders power the crane that hoists the steel plates into position.
(*Source:* National Archives, U.S. Army Signal Corps.)

these things and just say to yourself, 'Tsk! I couldn't describe all these things!' There were so many things that we had not seen before . . . simply did not know what they were" (Ngwadili et al. 1988, 211).

The often nonchalant treatment of their cargo on the part of military personnel was striking. Americans frequently gave away food rations, clothing, cutlery, blankets, and other miscellaneous supplies to local people. More amazing still, at the end of the war, vast amounts of supplies were bulldozed into the sea. It was easier to ditch the contents of island warehouses than to ship them home. There is more than one beach near the site of wartime supply bases, like Espiritu Santo's "million-dollar point," where skindivers today can swim through the remnants of sunken hoards alongside tropical reef fish. At Kukum docks, Guadalcanal, for example, the Army burned, buried, or dumped at sea 58,831 tons of cargo worth $19,888,587 at the end of the war (Stauffer 1956, 321).

The word *cargo* appeared again after the war to describe a series of political movements. These came into existence, in part, to protest the reestablishment of prewar colonial relations. In Melanesia, these movements were the infamous "cargo cults," so named because of islanders' common concern to acquire manufactured goods first encountered in great quantities during the war (see, e.g., Worsley 1968). Many cults and movements had been known before the 1940s. The war, however, sparked new demands for political autonomy and economic development throughout the Pacific. It broke through cramped horizons. From Tahiti to the Solomon Islands, islanders organized to achieve political and economic goals that were focused by their wartime experiences.

In some regions, cargo movements incorporated traditional religious beliefs about the importance of magical as well as technological knowledge for the production of goods. Here, people engaged in ritualistic behavior to obtain cargo: washing money, laying out and clearing runways in the forest, rearranging traditional marriages and other relations between men and women, ecstatic dancing, awaiting the return of the ancestors, talking to "America" via bamboo radio antennae or flower telephones—all this in a fervent quest for the cargo they had observed during the war.

Rumors still circulate around the Pacific of secret caches of cargo that the Americans left behind for their return someday. A veteran of the Solomon Islands Labour Corps, for example, describes this hidden cargo:

Those things still remain a secret. They said that they had hidden them for the next world war. There is a big town in the earth on Guadalcanal. The British and some other people have been trying to find it but they have not succeeded. The Americans dug big holes in the earth and then built big houses with cement. It is a big town. They took the big trucks, tanks and ammunition and put them in the houses (Ngwadili et al. 1988, 213).

Postwar cargo cults built on people's wartime experiences and aspirations. These aspirations, however, were often more complex than a simple desire to

Munda, New Georgia, Solomon Islands, February 1944. Two islanders use a new tool as they fill ditches in a manioc garden to control mosquitos. The Navy's release on the photograph notes, "Sailors later taught them the right way." (*Source:* National Archives, U.S. Navy.)

Noumea, New Caledonia, November 1942. Many islanders also learned to use more complex tools. Two New Caledonians use a tractor to move cargo about the Noumea docks. (*Source:* National Archives, U.S. Army Signal Corps.)

Lae, Papua New Guinea, December 1944.
Workers recruited by ANGAU discover assembly-line techniques as they operate bottle-washing equipment, boxing bottles for refilling at the Army Canteens Service soft drink factory.
(*Source:* Australian War Memorial.)

Banika, Russell Islands, Solomon Islands, January 1945. Military photographers often played with images of the war's technological impact on simple villagers. The original photo caption reads, "Big Eyes: South Pacific natives bring their knives to Marines of the largest supply base in the South Pacific to be sharpened and gaze in wonderment as the sparks fly off the emery wheel."
(*Source:* National Archives, U.S. Marine Corps.)

acquire the sorts of goods that were once piled high in wartime storage warehouses. Islanders were also concerned to acquire the technological *information* they knew lay behind cargo's production. The "cargo" in "cargo cult" meant something more than the ritualistic pursuit of mythic shopping lists. It symbolized, in shorthand, an initial realization of the power of industrial production, as well as a realization of the opportunities and dangers this technology entails for small island societies. After all, many islanders had personally observed, operated, and enjoyed manufactured goods before and during the war years. They had used cargo and, in some cases, had seen it assembled and even produced in military shops and storehouses. They had witnessed for the first time an entire modern technology in operation. This comprised a body of productive knowledge, new tools and complex machines, and an elaborate organization of military labor.

When islanders joined native labor corps or worked informally for either the Allies or the Japanese, they learned to use new tools ranging from simple shovels to bulldozers and heavy equipment. A photograph of two islanders *carrying* a wheelbarrow loaded with debris, instead of pushing it, constitutes an archetypal representation of this learning process. Work skills quickly developed, however. Photographs, for example, record New Caledonians driv-

Brisbane, Australia, November 1943.
Islanders from Japanese-held Irian Jaya (Dutch New Guinea) were taken to Brisbane by the Australian administration to witness firsthand the strength of Allied economies. Here they mount a tow motor lift to get a closer look at corned beef supplies. The hope was that these men, returning home, would convince their fellow villages to support the Allies vis-à-vis the Japanese. "Hearts and minds" was another use for wartime photography: "Proof of their tales will be given natives through photographs of tour." (*Source:* National Archives, U.S. Army Signal Corps.)

ing tractors around the Noumea docks, transporting incoming cargo. Other islanders had a crash course in intensive agriculture while working on military farms, whether those of the Japanese in Micronesia, or of the Allies in Melanesia.

Along with new skills, a few people obtained direct, firsthand exposure to the industrial technology that lay behind the war machines. The Allies flew several groups of islanders from Papua New Guinea and Irian Jaya to factories in Australia, so that they might observe close at hand the details of wartime mass production. Captions on the pictures that Army photographers took of the tour note:

Natives were brought here to view installations so that they may get a picture of Allied might. Object: to so impress the natives that, through their influence and the recording of their experiences, native tribes of Dutch New Guinea may be induced to afford the fullest co-operation to Allied troops entering that territory. Proofs of their stories, in the form of photos depicting various stages of their trip, will be furnished visiting natives.

Here was another use of wartime photography.

Military supply lines thus carried more than materiel into Pacific isles. Those lines extended modern, industrialized forms of production and distribution into an undeveloped economic hinterland. Many islanders themselves played small but critical roles within the new martial economy. In doing so, they learned to appreciate something of the system as a whole as well as its various products. Winning battles required complex secondary technologies to transport goods and people and to communicate information.

Brisbane, Australia, November 1943.
The tourists, wearing new military uniforms, take a look at 50 cal. machine guns. The sponsors of the tour hoped that at least three of the islanders were "native chieftains."
(*Source:* National Archives, U.S. Army Signal Corps.)

Guadalcanal, Solomon
Islands, August 1943.
Weaponry was the deadliest
of the new technologies
that islanders encountered
during the war. In this photo,
islanders employed at a coastwatching station stop up
their ears as an antiaircraft
gun is fired. The gun's crew is
protected from low-flying
planes by the machine gun in
pit at the right.
(*Source:* National Archives,
U.S. Army Signal Corps.)

Combat

The machines of war were striking and fearsome. Here, the product was
death. Warships and cargo vessels (which some islanders learned to call
"mailboats") sailed waters that, before 1942, had mostly known only copra
boats. Tank-carrying ships, as on Nissan Island, appeared at landing passages
where previously only canoes had drawn ashore. PT-boats—one of the fastest
military vessels ever built—awed Solomon Islanders accustomed to paddling between islands. War planes flew in skies where no airplane had flown
before and landed in great numbers at newly leveled airfields. On Segond
Canal, Espiritu Santo, and throughout the Solomons, amphibious planes
such as Catalinas, Kingfishers, and Ducks splashed down on waters shared
with traditional sailing canoes. Islanders observed these aerial maneuvers
and, occasionally, even accepted invitations to fly.

More lethal sorts of military technology also came ashore across Pacific
beaches. Ordnance of all sorts—tanks, ammunition, bombs, machine guns,

Above: **Nissan (Green) Island, February 1944.**
The war introduced various new means of transport that impressed many islanders. Tank landing ships come ashore on a small Pacific atoll.
(*Source:* National Archives, U.S. Marine Corps.)

Right: **Lake Sentani, Irian Jaya (Dutch New Guinea), April 1944.**
Villagers living on the shores of Lake Sentani paddle out to, according to the original caption, "surrender" to U.S. amphibious "Buffaloes."
(*Source:* National Archives, U.S. Army Signal Corps.)

antiaircraft guns, artillery—was shipped into the Pacific. Islanders quickly developed an appreciation for some of this weaponry, particularly hand grenades and dynamite. In the Solomons, Army Engineers "found them using hand grenades to kill fish, and cooking them in an oven made out of belly-tanks jettisoned from airplanes" (Van Dusen 1945, 32). When caught between the warring forces, however, islanders suffered the deadly power of their weapons. To this day, sizeable areas of beach and forest remain off limits on some islands due to large numbers of unexploded shells. The return of military bomb squads to assist with postwar cleanup operations is a continuing reminder of the war's deadly cargo.

Transportation

Islander encounters with other kinds of military technology were a more welcome experience. Perhaps the most popular technological innovations the war brought to the Pacific region were those that enhanced travel. Voyagers with rich, traditional navigational skills had settled these islands. In some Pacific regions, people continued to sail canoes to distant lands. American

Kwai, Malaita, Solomon Islands, June 1943. First of its kind to land in this area, a U.S. Navy "Duck" seaplane fascinates village children. Many islanders also remember the surprise they felt when first seeing amphibious motor vehicles at work at military ports. (*Source:* National Archives, U.S. Navy.)

and Japanese ships and airplanes facilitated this inter-island travel. At the Allied base at Milne Bay, for example, an ordnance plant nicknamed "Little Detroit" assembled up to 120 vehicles a day, while 2,000 landing craft were constructed at a nearby boat assembly plant (Nelson 1980b, 251–52).

Technological improvements in transportation were lauded in the messages of a number of postwar cults: cargo stories suggested that new goods would arrive by plane or by submarine. In fact, after the war, civilian aeronautics and shipping both made good use of the airfields and docks the retiring military forces left in place.

In addition to inter-island travel improvements, military engineers routed many miles of new roads, much improving local transportation systems. Kalaunapa of Efate Island, for example, recollects the amazement he felt when first seeing a bulldozer at work: "We saw the bulldozers coming. Before, there was nothing like it. When the bulldozers came, it was like a hurricane. All the trees just fell over . . . When we saw the bulldozers we said, 'That's not man. Only God can work like that!'" Jeeps and trucks carried men and cargo up and down these new roads. Islanders soon learned to stick out their thumbs; many became champion hitchhikers. At some bases, engineers built even more exotic means of transportation. Seabees on Guadalcanal laid a 1.22-mile-long "Guadalcanal-Bougainville-Tokyo" railroad. Photographs capture an admiring local audience at its completion ceremonies. On the other side of the battle lines, the Japanese army imported bicycles for its troops. As the Japanese pulled back from their positions throughout the Pacific, islanders frequently picked up abandoned vehicles and the skills to use them.

Lae area, Papua New Guinea, October 1943.
Island workers and Allied military men struggle to offload machinery at the Nadzab airstrip for the drive on Lae, about twenty miles downriver. Villagers must have wondered at the sudden appearance of fleets of planes that disgorged all kinds of supplies, weapons, and equipment.
(*Source:* Australian War Memorial.)

Cape Gloucester, New Britain, Papua New Guinea, January 1944.
Local men inspect the first U.S. plane to land at a new airport. Many islanders took their first plane ride during the war.
(*Source:* National Archives, U.S. Marine Corps.)

Hansa Bay, Papua New Guinea, June 1944.
Two New Guineans try their hand at starting an abandoned Japanese motorcycle as an Australian military man looks on. Many islanders learned how to drive during the war—frequently with surplus or abandoned vehicles, including motorcycles, jeeps, trucks, tractors, and even bulldozers.
(*Source:* Australian War Memorial.)

Guadalcanal, Solomon Islands, August 1943.
The first and only railroad on Guadalcanal is completed as the Commander of Naval Bases in the Solomons drives in the final spike. Just 1.2 miles in length, the "Guadalcanal-Bougainville-Tokyo" railroad took only three days to construct by Navy Seabees and the Solomon Islands Labour Corps, shown here watching the ceremony.
(*Source:* National Archives, U.S. Marine Corps.)

Communications

World War II observed the first full-scale deployment of new communicative technologies in the Pacific, such as radar and radio links. In Vanuatu, technicians occasionally invited islanders to observe radar operations. The locals were fascinated with a "glass" that could spy out enemy forces operating over the horizon. Some still insist that the "steal" (their pidgin English word for radar and air raid sirens combined) was powerful enough to detect Japanese ships and planes leaving Tokyo itself. In the Solomon Islands, where islanders worked at coastwatching stations, shortwave radios became familiar and occasionally life-saving devices. The military imported other technological marvels to process and circulate information. One photograph captures Solomon Islander war hero Jacob Vouza being interviewed in front of a typewriter. As bases developed, complex telephone networks were established. On Guadalcanal and Efate, island workers—expert coconut-palm climbers—helped draw the wires from pole to pole. On Guam, local women were hired to operate the military's telephone exchange.

Islanders also encountered other new media that transmitted information about the war back home to Japan and America. These included photography, cinematic filming, and tape-recording. Many people had their photographs taken for the first time. In the 1960s, anthropologist Lola Romanucci-Ross encountered a Manus man who still carefully preserved a picture of himself standing next to General MacArthur. Many, also for the first time,

Guadalcanal, Solomon Islands, June 1943. Modern military bases required the latest in communications technologies. Here Solomon Islands workers assist with the construction of Guadalcanal's first telephone system. (*Source:* National Archives, U.S. Marine Corps.)

Wildman River(?), Papua New Guinea, November 1943. An island scout looks on as an Australian intelligence officer uses a radio set while on patrol. (*Source:* National Museum of Victoria.)

Wewak, Papua New Guinea, July 1945.
The leader of an ANGAU "supply train" receives further orders by telephone. His carriers arrived twenty minutes behind Australian assault troops attacking a Japanese position nicknamed "The Blot."
(*Source:* Australian War Memorial.)

Guadalcanal, Solomon Islands, January 1943.
A Navy photographer explains an aerial camera to an interested islander. The war provided many opportunities to learn about and use new tools. The islander pictured also wears what was probably his first wristwatch.
(*Source:* National Archives, U.S. Navy.)

heard their voices recorded on tape, or listened as servicemen played records on phonographs.

Other communicative technologies served to inform and entertain the troops. At a number of American bases, local radio stations went on the air. From Radio Munda, Radio Guam, and others, choirs drawn from village populations, labor corps, and local defense forces performed for military radio audiences. Base newspapers were also established. Perhaps the most famous of these was Papua New Guinea's *Guinea Gold*. At Port Moresby, islanders who had previously worked for the colonial printing office were employed as linotype operators, compositors, letterpress machinists, and table hands for this newspaper that is estimated to have had a readership of eight hundred

Port Moresby, Papua New Guinea, August 1944. Seura Dai of Hanuabada Village is pictured with his equipment for making metal casts of the comic strips "Blondie" and "Popeye" for the military daily newspaper *Guinea Gold*.
(*Source:* National Archives, U.S. Army Signal Corps.)

thousand (Wallace 1971). These men, including a displaced Caroline Islander, continued to work on the newspaper after it moved, following the front, to Lae and then to Rabaul.

Cinema also came to the Pacific. Islanders occasionally were the subjects of both Allied and Japanese propaganda films and newsreels. In addition to being filmed themselves, they also sat beside servicemen to watch Hollywood films, some of them about the war. In September 1944, one army chaplain organized a combined organ concert and movie showing for islanders at Houailou, New Caledonia—"the first time any of them had seen a movie." After playing a few hymns on a portable Hammond organ loaded on a trailer, he screened Donald Duck and the film *King of Kings*. In Vanuatu's pidgin English today, animated cartoons have come to be called "Miki," after Mickey Mouse. Most large bases had numerous movie screens where a variety of

Oro Bay, Papua New Guinea, October 1944.
Many islanders saw their first movies and newsreels at base theaters. An islander carries sandwich boards to advertise the premiere of *Dragon Seed*.
(*Source:* National Archives, U.S. Army Signal Corps.)

films were shown. Espiritu Santo reportedly had forty-three. The war introduced to the Pacific new technologies to store, deploy, and transmit information, and the faces of islanders are discernible today among all of the wartime words, images, and voices these media captured.

Pacific islanders observed and handled tons of cargo throughout the course of World War II. This cargo has had lasting effects. Much of it, in fact, is still out there—and not only underwater at "million-dollar points." Quonset huts remain in good use near Lungga Point, Guadalcanal and also at the site of the naval hospital at Bellevue Plantation, Efate. Unexploded bombs surface in people's gardens. Wreckage and other war relics have been gathered into war museums, and some also decorate public spaces. Jeeps, even, are still today occasionally offered for sale in the want ads of island newspapers.

More significantly, by handling cargo, many islanders thereby encountered and learned to work within an unfamiliar technological order as they were drawn into the military economy. The war's cargo was to be used. It was imported to produce victory. Islanders laid down heavy sheets of steel Marsden matting on runways, worked in motor pool repair shops, drove tractors, operated telephone exchanges, mastered wheelbarrows and hitchhiking, flew to Australia to visit war production facilities, performed on radio, typeset comic strips like "Popeye" and "Blondie," rode motorcycles and amphibious vehicles and, of course, had their pictures taken. These technological experiences were also part of the war's cargo, and their effects have lasted in memories of the vast riches of war.

**Nggela(?) (Florida Islands),
Solomon Islands, August 1943.
Doctors examine children at
a Solomon Islands base hospital. Many military doctors
treated islanders in addition
to sick and wounded troops.**
(*Source:* National Archives,
U.S. Navy.)

7. Medicine

War keeps doctors employed. One of the most influential technologies the combatants brought into the Pacific was modern Japanese and Western medicine. Some of this medical practice, of course, was known in the region before the war. Japanese doctors worked in Micronesia; European and American colonial governments, and Christian missions elsewhere, funded hospitals and public health programs. Much of this medical establishment, however, served expatriates. Military medicine, too, was imported primarily to serve the troops—to heal the wounded, cure the sick, and maintain a healthy fighting force in general. The purview of Army and Navy medical corps, however, soon broadened to include various segments of island populations. In some regions, nearly everyone became the patients of the military.

The war brought together two large populations: Pacific islanders on the one hand, and Allied and Japanese servicemen on the other. In many Pacific areas, military doctors soon warned that local villagers provided large "pools" or "reservoirs" for mosquito-borne diseases such as malaria and filariasis (elephantiasis). In actuality, transmission of illness flowed two ways. Each population was a reservoir of disease that, potentially, could endanger the other. Military personnel came down with malaria, dengue fever, and scrub typhus; islanders, for their part, were infected with measles, chicken pox, and pneumonia. In the Papua New Guinea central highlands where people were otherwise minimally affected by the war, a dysentery epidemic moved rapidly through dense populations, killing perhaps ten thousand people (Nelson 1980b, 252).

The need to safeguard the health of the troops generated research into endemic tropical diseases including malaria, filariasis, and yaws (a skin disease) (e.g., Parsons 1945). Before the war, scientific knowledge of these Pacific diseases was spotty at best. Large concentrations of troops encouraged the

115

Guam, 1942.
The Japanese military also provided medical care to islanders in the regions it occupied. Japanese physicians and Chamorro nurses treat local children on Guam. (*Source:* Kyuya Takenaka.)

application of widescale public health measures and the development of new medicines to control, if not conquer, tropical afflictions. Furthermore, public health programs directed treatment toward local populations as well, to reduce the threat of endemic Pacific diseases being transmitted to the troops. As much as any aspect of Western knowledge and technology, the efficiency of modern medicines and medical practices left deep impressions upon islander sensibilities that persist to the present time.

It was malaria, in particular, that caused military medical care to spill over to islanders. Early in the war, seriously high rates of malarial infection at bases such as Milne Bay and Efate convinced military medical corps that the mosquito was deadlier than the enemy. Early in 1943, Australian and American battle casualties in Papua numbered 7,752. Casualties from tropical diseases, however, totaled 37,360, including 27,892 cases of malaria alone. Entire divisions were infected with the disease. In Vanuatu, rates of infection at Efate in April 1942 reached 2,675 per 1,000 men per year. Infection rates among the Australians at Milne Bay were even higher. They topped out at 4,264 per 1,000 per year. At this rate, the Australians estimated that their fighting force would fall to zero in three months (Walker 1957, 116).

Military medical officers instituted a number of prophylactic measures that quickly lowered malarial infection rates, including distribution of sleeping nets, orders to wear long shirts and pants after sunset, prohibitions on visits to local plantations and villages, filling and oiling of sources of standing water to destroy mosquito breeding grounds, and mass treatment of troops with atabrine, the most available malaria prophylactic. The Japanese had taken Java and occupied other important sources of the antimalarial drug quinine. Atabrine (or quinacrine) is derived principally from acridine, a crystalline component of coal tar. In highly malarial areas, troops were given

Merizo, Guam, November 1944.
After the Americans recaptured the island, a pharmacist's mate treats the infected hand of a young Chamorro girl in a Navy dispensary constructed of local material.
(*Source:* National Archives, U.S. Navy.)

Dobodura, Papua New Guinea, February 1943. Many labor corps workers became ill and sometimes died from inadequate diets, long working days, or introduced disease. In this photo, members of ANGAU (Australian New Guinea Administrative Unit) labor corps receive treatment at a hospital set aside for islanders. In addition to Australian doctors, care was provided by trained local medical practitioners.
(*Source:* National Archives, U.S. Army Signal Corps.)

Nggela (Florida Islands), Solomon Islands, August 1943. The war directed medical attention to several endemic Pacific diseases, especially yaws and malaria. During the war, many islanders received medication for these diseases for the first time. In this photo, a Seabee doctor prepares to give a yaws injection to a young boy at Halavo Seaplane Base.
(*Source:* National Archives, U.S. Navy.)

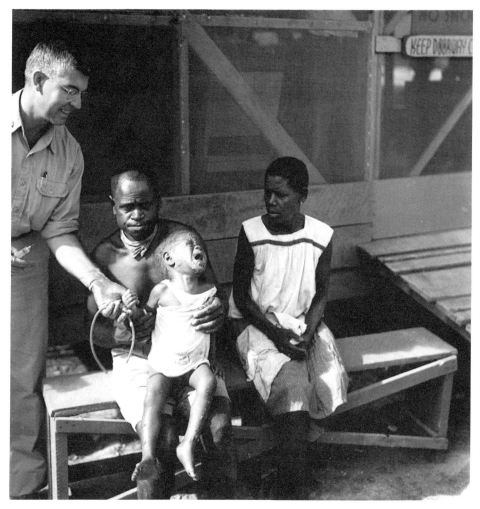

a dosage twice weekly. The drug was known, after several months, to turn the skin yellowish. Soldiers suspected it of having a number of more serious side effects, more along the lines of saltpeter. Local grass-skirt and artifact makers much appreciated it as a yellow dye; James Michener's story of Atabrine Benny and Bloody Mary records something of the unofficial trafficking in the drug (Michener 1947).

Suppressive malaria therapy at some bases was extended to local populations in addition to military personnel. Surveys on Efate indicated that endemic malarial rates varied from 10 to 52 percent in different parts of the island. Mass treatment was given to the great majority of islanders. After treatment, blood parasite rates fell dramatically (Butler 1943, 1608). The military's need for an effective fighting force improved, as a consequence, the health of its island hosts.

In addition to receiving medication, many Pacific islanders also took part in mosquito control efforts. Large amounts of local labor were required to fill and drain ditches and ruts in order to eliminate surface water suitable for mosquito breeding, or to convert water sources into faster running channels. Around the Pacific, islanders dug miles of drainage ditches, installed culverts and dams, excavated massive sump holes, cleared, channelled, and sometimes altered the course of streams, all to eliminate standing water. Other islanders were organized into spraying squads to coat waters suitable for mosquito breeding with thin films of diesel oil no. 2. By the end of 1942, five hundred islanders were at work draining and eliminating forty square miles of mosquito breeding grounds at Milne Bay.

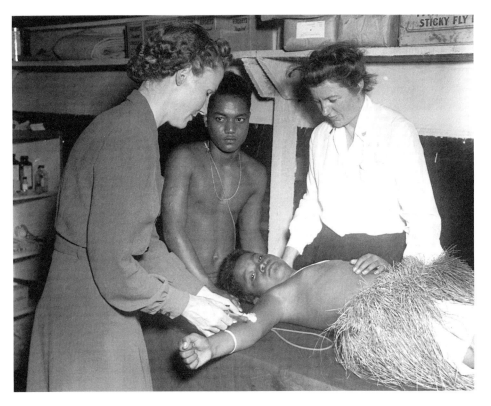

Fassarai, Ulithi, Federated States of Micronesia, April 1945.
Navy nurses give a yaws injection to a Micronesian child. Ugly skin ulcerations and bone lesions made yaws one of the most obvious medical problems in the Pacific. Yaws virtually disappeared thanks to the military's antibiotics and innoculation campaigns. The effectiveness of these treatments convinced many islanders of the power of Western medicine, particularly when administered through injections.
(*Source:* National Archives, U.S. Navy.)

Majuro, Marshall Islands, June 1944.
A Navy doctor and his eleven-year-old nurse, nicknamed "Peanuts," give an injection on Majuro.
(*Source:* National Archives, U.S. Marine Corps.)

Aside from the mass treatment of local populations to control endemic tropical diseases, islanders received other kinds of care from military doctors. Hospitals were built across the Pacific. A U.S. doctor assigned to help establish a naval hospital in Samoa described a scene that was repeated at bases all over the Pacific: "the Seabees—the CAN DO boys—arrived in a caravan of trucks, pitched their tents in our park and went to work. Buildings sprang up like mushrooms and in a few days we had no more worries about bed capacity" (Parsons 1945, 102). One of the hospitals at Milne Bay had beds for six thousand patients (Nelson 1980b, 252). In some places, the military established native clinics. On New Georgia, for example, doctors treated patients for ringworm, common throughout the Southwest Pacific before the war. On Tonga, Army medics conducted first-aid and sanitation courses in Tongan villages in order to reduce the case load at the Army's newly constructed 750-bed hospital (Weeks 1987).

Where native labor corps were established, good health programs kept workers on the job. Along with military personnel, labor corps members were dosed regularly with atabrine. They also received care for other ailments and injuries. Medical officers were assigned to labor corps units in the Solomon Islands, Papua New Guinea, and Vanuatu. Native medical orderlies and practitioners, some trained at Fiji's well-known native medical college, also provided treatment to the sick and to workers injured on the job.

During the initial years of the war, care was sometimes inadequate. Only a few doctors were available to treat carriers along the Kokoda Trail in Papua

Bougainville, Papua New Guinea, February 1944. New public health measures were developed during the war to reduce massive troop casualties from malaria. In this photograph, young "spraymen" apply a fuel mixture on stagnant waters to kill mosquito larvae. The original caption of the photo reports, **"Their pay is the food provided them by the Service Mess."**

(*Source:* National Archives, U.S. Navy.)

Espiritu Santo, Vanuatu (New Hebrides), September 1943.
By controlling malarial infection levels among Pacific islanders, military doctors hoped to protect servicemen. Health teams attacked mosquitos in villages located near bases with "freon bombs."
(*Source:* National Archives, U.S. Navy.)

Espiritu Santo, Vanuatu (New Hebrides), September 1943.
Local populations were dosed weekly with the malaria prophylactic atabrine. A doctor in the background of this photo palpates the spleen of an islander; an enlarged spleen is a common symptom of malarial infection.
(*Source:* National Archives, U.S. Navy.)

during the 1942 fighting. The following year, on paper ANGAU had assigned 306 native medical assistants and orderlies to treat its thousands of workers; in actuality, only 142 were on the job (Ryan 1969, 543). Many workers fell ill or were caught in action and wounded or killed. Dysentery and beriberi were particularly troublesome in the labor corps. Workers presumed the change in diet—novel tinned meats and fats—was responsible for the common "runny belly," or dysentery, they experienced. Early in the war, cases of beriberi—a thiamine deficiency—were discovered among workers in Papua New Guinea, the Solomons, and Vanuatu. Military doctors attributed this to polished rice issued to workers. Cases of beriberi decreased when supply officers ordered unpolished rice for labor corps meals.

Members of local defense forces, scouting units, and coastwatching camps also received first aid and hospital care if wounded in action. Many were. The Papuan Infantry Regiment lost, officially, 110 of its members wounded in action, 43 killed in action, 64 dying otherwise, and 11 missing, presumed killed (Robinson 1981, 190). The Papua New Guinea native police force lost 91 members. Some wounded islanders found their way into military hospitals where they received treatment. A number of photographs record islanders being fitted with prostheses to replace missing arms and legs. Army Engineers and Seabees, in particular, were skilled at constructing artificial limbs out of odd bits of equipment they scavenged around their bases.

The military also treated—often unofficially—islanders who were not members of labor corps or defense forces. A man from New Britain, for ex-

Ongtong Java, Solomon Islands, 1945.
A Navy doctor palpates the spleen of a woman on a small Polynesian atoll, north of the Solomons.
(*Source:* National Archives, U.S. Navy.)

Koil Island, Papua New Guinea, October 1945. Women line up to have their spleens palpated by an ANGAU doctor on a Red Cross medical inspection tour.
(*Source:* Australian War Memorial.)

ample, recalls that, as a young boy, he had his arm nearly severed when a shell he was throwing rocks at exploded. An Australian medic at a nearby aid post was ready to amputate his arm, but the American Marine who had brought him in protested that the loss of an arm would ruin his life. The Marine took him by patrol boat to a hospital sixty miles away where American doctors saved his arm (Counts 1989). The availability of medicines and modern hospital equipment, the charity and generosity of medical personnel, and the opportunity to practice one's calling on unique tropical diseases and conditions led many doctors to treat local people freely. At some hospitals, doctors were able to do so only by "forgetting" orders not to extend care to non-military personnel. Occasionally, doctors encountered conditions they rarely saw back home. The highlight of more than one surgeon's tour of duty was the opportunity to operate on a victim of elephantiasis of the scrotum.

The confusion and disruption of battle had serious public health consequences. When the Americans occupied Micronesia, they discovered a local population that had had little access to medical care during the war years. Many people were suffering from yaws. The military stationed doctors on various Micronesian atolls, such as Ulithi, to stabilize the yaws epidemic and to treat people with other illnesses. Elsewhere, treatment was directed to more specific categories of patients. Military doctors regularly examined women at Noumea's notorious Pink Palace and also a population of well-known ladies on Tonga, in order to control the spread of venereal disease.

In the short term, the war had obvious deleterious effects on island health; many people were killed, wounded, or fell victim to endemic or alien dis-

New Georgia, Solomon Islands, December 1943. Military physicians also treated common Pacific skin diseases. An islander receives ringworm medication while standing in a cabinet made from an old x-ray developing unit at a Navy native health clinic.
(*Source:* National Archives, U.S. Navy.)

eases. The war years, nevertheless, were a medical threshold. As with transportation, communication, and other technologies, the modernization of medical practice in the Pacific can be traced in large measure to World War II. Tropical diseases such as malaria, filiariasis, and scrub typhus were, for the first time, attended to on a large scale. Some of these diseases, such as yaws, would soon be essentially eliminated.

The war had other long-term medical effects. Many islanders received training as medical orderlies, practitioners, and dressers. They also became acquainted with public health and sanitation measures, particularly those important for mosquito control. Many of the hospitals put up initially as a collection of Quonset huts to tend the sick and wounded continue to operate at their old military addresses—such as "No. 9," the largest hospital in the

Cape Gloucester, New Britain, Papua New Guinea, September 1944.
Many islanders were wounded when caught between battling forces. This man lost a leg during the American invasion of Cape Gloucester, but received a carved mahogany one in return from an Army Engineer.
(*Source:* National Archives, U.S. Army Signal Corps.)

Solomon Islands. The war contributed to the medical infrastructures of newly independent island nations. Alongside new buildings, new attitudes about medicine that the war introduced also still prevail. Although most Pacific islanders today continue to practice systems of traditional medicine, because of the war they also entertain a fondness for "stick medicine" (injections) and other aspects of Western medicine.

Tutuba, Vanuatu (New Hebrides), August 1943. Titus Molirani, sporting a sailor's hat and a necklace of traditional shell money, submits to a dental examination by military dentists from the nearby American base on Espiritu Santo.
(*Source:* National Archives, U.S. Navy.)

**Peleliu, Palau, October 1944.
American Civil Affairs officer
makes friends by giving
candy to children after the
Marines' amphibious landing
on the island.**
(*Source:* National Archives,
U.S. Marine Corps.)

8. Exchange

The official price for bananas in wartime Tonga was 164 pounds for a dollar (Weeks 1987, 425). That was a lot of bananas for the money, even in 1942 dollars. More important, the fact that the American military established on Tonga a system of fixed prices—as it did elsewhere around the Pacific—signifies something of the magnitude of trading, bartering, and exchanging instigated by the war. Dollars (and yen) flooded small Pacific communities, rolling through once sickly plantation economies depressed by low tropical commodity prices and by the war's disruptive effects on shipping.

Throughout the Pacific, the act of exchanging goods is imbued with wider social meaning. In the Polynesian Islands, where there are chiefs and commoners, a chief's status and power are symbolized and upheld by his generosity. The flow of goods between a chief and his subjects legitimizes his sovereignty. In Melanesia, where positions of leadership are generally achieved rather than inherited, people's political fortunes depend in large part upon their management of feasts and other exchanges. A leader and his supporters must give away large amounts of food and other goods to their kin and political allies. By exchanging goods, two people (or two groups) demonstrate their friendship and mutual support. One initial act of exchange can bring into being lifelong political alliances.

On the American side, servicemen quickly earned a reputation for generosity or, from a different perspective, extravagance. Some of this generosity, at least, must be understood in light of the fact that much of what servicemen gave away was U.S. taxpayer–supplied military property. It is perhaps not surprising that the contents of poorly inventoried warehouses and storerooms were raided with a light heart. American veterans today tell stories of their playful attempts to sink island canoes with bags of rice as the canoes pulled up alongside naval vessels for trade, and of discovering that most of

**Panaeati, Louisiade Archi-
pelago, Papua New Guinea,
n.d.
Japanese officers and islanders exchange presents.**
(*Source: Mainichi Shimbun.*)

the bed linen on a ship had been given away at the last port of call. On Tonga, American gifts to island friends included generators, carburetors, radios, ice-boxes, and beer. One petty officer built an entire house for his Tongan girl-friend using American equipment and supplies (Weeks 1987).

Motivations for giving things away on the part of Allied and Japanese troops ranged from genuine compassion and concern for islanders made refugees by battle to the carefree distribution of cigarettes, food, clothing, and other goods by servicemen at supply bases who had more than enough for themselves. Peculiar cross-cultural, wartime misunderstandings arose from these different meanings and practices of giving. Garbage is a case in point. Americans understand garbage in a certain way. The material and trash left behind in dumps when bases were rolled up was just that—useless stuff thrown away. At least some Pacific islanders concluded differently: this material had been left behind *for them.*

Islanders invariably compared these gifts and this generosity with the more parsimonious exchanges that characterized their prewar relations with planters and traders. In comparison with these European colonials, generous giving during the war transformed servicemen into something akin to Polynesian chiefs, or Melanesian friends and allies. Colonial authorities often attempted to contain the flow of surplus military supplies into native hands lest they engender expectations that would make difficult the reestablishment of labor relations after the war. A Solomon Islander recalls his disappointment at these policies: "An official of the Protectorate Government . . . did his best to stop the armed forces from giving free supplies to the local people. Villagers were told not to accept gifts from the soldiers. It was heartbreaking to see surplus mosquito nets, bedding and foodstuffs dumped into the sea while they were so badly needed by the general population" (Zoleveke 1980, 26).

Abaotau, Tarawa, Kiribati (Gilbert Islands), June 1944. Gift-giving during the war flowed two ways, and many islanders recall the presents they gave the Allied and Japanese servicemen. Just six months after the devastating U.S. invasion of Tarawa, these islanders offer a token of goodwill to the Allies. (*Source:* Fiji Ministry of Information.)

Abemama, Kiribati (Gilbert Islands), June 1944. Islanders contributed to both Allied and Japanese war funds. In this photograph, people from Abemama donate money (American dollars, in this case) to Britain's war fund. (*Source:* Fiji Ministry of Information.)

Exchange of objects between Pacific islanders and Allied and Japanese servicemen ranged from the noncalculative giving of presents, to barter, to the sale of goods and services for money in the new marketplaces and stalls that sprung up around military establishments: the casual gift of cigarettes, candy, or chewing gum to local children on one end of this continuum and the haggling over the price of a pig's tusk or grass skirt at the other. Gift giving, or the nonmonetary sort of transaction, more closely resembled traditional exchange in the Pacific. This wartime liberality is what Pacific islanders remember and recount today. Michael Somare, for example, recalls in his autobiography the generosity of Japanese troops after their landing on the north coast of New Guinea (1975): "They quickly made friends with our people. They brought many presents of food, clothes and all sorts of good things, and they passed around plenty of whiskey. So our people had a big celebration on the arrival of the Japanese."

Parallel accounts of American generosity are common on the other side of the battle lines. A Solomon Islander from Malaita, describing the arrival of American troops, recalls:

They came with their cargo and you ate until you could not eat anymore so you threw the food away. When the boxes would break open and food would fall out of them all over the place, we would not take it because we were afraid as we had never stolen anything before. But the Americans said, "You all eat these things. This is our food. Let us all eat while we are all still alive" (Ngwadili et al. 1988, 208).

Ailinglapalap, Marshall Islands, June 1944.
Wartime gift-giving sometimes occurred during formal ceremonies. Islanders make a presentation of woven baskets, hats, mats, drinking coconuts, and other gifts to a party of visiting Navy officers.
(*Source:* National Archives, U.S. Navy.)

Similarly, an older man from the island of Nguna in Vanuatu recollects:

Before, we had no good roads. The Americans came and worked on a big road around all of Efate. And they took us to go help them with this work. They looked after us well. They transported us to Vila so that we might get many things—sugar, rice, or many other things. And they took us free, and brought us back again free. Their launches brought us to our land. They were truly our good friends. When they were to go back, they gave us many things. They gave us many clothes, lumber for houses, much iron. And they helped us with those things that we didn't have before. And I remember one time a good man gave a hundred dollars to help our District School. Some came and gave us injections. When we went to shake hands with them [say farewell], many from Nguna loved them very much. And they loved us very much (Schütz 1968, 312).

These wartime gift exchanges were not entirely unidirectional. Not all goods flowed from servicemen to islanders. Exchange in the Pacific is properly reciprocal. The alliances and friendships created by exchange of goods entail responsibilities on both sides. A person's honor and good name depend on giving gifts to balance gifts received. Islanders and servicemen exchanged informal gifts and services (lighting each other's cigarettes, for example) and, occasionally, formally traded presents, such as Adm. Chester Nimitz's gift of cigarettes and other supplies to the people of Ailinglapalap and their return gifts of baskets and woven hats. These sorts of exchanges challenged prewar colonial codes that served to maintain distinctions between islanders and settlers. Wartime commensalism and giving contrasted with previous pat-

Ailinglapalap, Marshall Islands, June 1944.
In return, "in the name of Admiral Nimitz," the Naval officers present islanders with a pile of military supplies including cigarettes, cigars, spools of thread, knives, and caramel candy.
(*Source:* National Archives, U.S. Navy.)

terns of exchange that purposely accentuated the inequality and separation of islanders and Europeans.

Islanders today are concerned to emphasize that they gave as well as received. They point to the fact that they participated economically in the war effort (on both sides). They contributed labor, garden produce, and other goods to both the Allies and the Japanese. Thus, Michael Somare goes on to note that when the Japanese retreated, local people wept and prepared smoked fish for them to take along (Somare 1970, 31). The Ngunese elder reports that Americans "needed bananas, pineapple, sugarcane, chicken, and everything. We brought many things for them, and gave them to them . . . We were happy that we were able to help them with everything of the land" (Schütz 1968, 311).

In some Pacific countries, islanders contributed to organized fund drives to support the war. In Japanese Micronesia, people on the island of Palau donated 131,815 yen (approximately $560) in 1943 to a war fund campaign (Higuchi 1986, 21). (For comparison, in 1940 Palauan miners earned less than one yen per day.) In Tonga, by holding bazaars and dances throughout the war, islanders raised enough money to buy three Spitfires for the British Royal Air Force. In Fiji, the Indian population raised enough money to buy a bomber named the *Fiji Indian.*

Alongside the giving and receiving of gifts and war contributions, the war sparked increased market exchange as well. Military paymasters disbursed dollars and yen for servicemen's pay, labor corps wages, rents, and reparation payments. (Even coconut trees had their price.) Dollars and yen supplanted francs and shillings in much of the Pacific. As the Japanese retreated, islanders exchanged yen for dollars with souveniring American servicemen. These currency influxes produced both a seller's market and inflation in small is-

Opposite: **Munda, New Georgia, Solomon Islands, October 1943.
Napatali Bea (left) and Ben Avualvulu (right) enjoy "C" ration biscuits given to them by U.S. troops. Giving away surplus food and goods earned Americans a reputation for generosity in many parts of the Pacific. Sharing food is especially important in Pacific cultures as a symbol of close relations and mutual trust.**
(*Source:* National Archives, U.S. Navy.)

Left: **Ukilim, Papua New Guinea, May 1944.
Gifts and exchanges of food were common throughout the war. Both islanders and servicemen appreciated new items in their diet. In this photograph, islanders load up a barge with papayas, bananas, and other produce from their gardens. Under a bartering agreement with the Australian Army Service Corps, every week islanders swapped a load of local fruits and vegetables for army rations.**
(*Source:* Australian War Memorial.)

Espiritu Santo, Vanuatu (New Hebrides), January 1943. Sailors buy pineapples and bananas from an islander trading out of his outrigger canoe.
(*Source:* National Archives, U.S. Navy.)

land economies. At some bases, recently paid servicemen consumers, searching for something—anything—to buy, far outnumbered sellers in the marketplace.

The concentration of troops created an economic demand for new services (restaurants, laundries, casual labor) and goods (fruits and other island foods to supplement military menus, home-brewed alcoholic drinks such as "jungle juice" or "torpedo juice," and souvenirs). European settlers and, in New Caledonia and Vanuatu, Vietnamese plantation workers met much of this demand—establishing restaurants, laundries, and market stalls in which they sold food and curios. Pacific islanders, too, responded to new market opportunities by going into business as wage laborers and petty traders. A Catholic priest in the Solomon Islands noted in his diary in May 1943 that he observed "a whole fleet of native canoes travelling toward Lunga to trade with the American soldiers." Sir Frederick Osifelo, a fourteen-year-old boy on Malaita in 1942, recalls the effects of the new market for artifacts in his area:

> The demand by American Marine and Army personnel for such things as sea-shells, carvings, walking-sticks, grass skirts, combs and so on, resulted in even people of my age focussing on making or finding something to sell. I was fourteen years old in 1942/1943 and actively involved in making walking-sticks, combs and grass skirts. At night we went out to the reef with torches or lit coconut leaves in search of sea-shells. Sometimes we sent our stuff to Lunga with relatives working in the Labour Corps so that they could sell them for us; at other times we sold them ourselves when the warships visited Auki (Osifelo 1985, 23).

The military and colonial powers attempted to regulate the war's economy. Colonial governments were especially concerned to control inflation, fearful of servicemen's abilities to outbid settlers in purchasing local goods and hiring local labor. At most bases, military authorities attempted to fix both

Mendaropu, Papua New Guinea, October 1942. The demand by military personnel for souvenirs created a whole industry of "tourist arts" in areas where few outsiders had traveled before the war. In this photograph, villagers barter tapa cloth—characteristic of Oro Province—with an officer of ANGAU. (*Source:* Australian War Memorial.)

Apia, Western Samoa, January 1944.

Many islanders quickly became aware of the trade potential of their traditional arts. They also learned to produce those items most favored by the troops, especially grass skirts, walking sticks, and models of sailing canoes. In port towns with military bases, vendors regularly plied their wares to base personnel. Here a U.S. military policeman bargains with a Samoan woman.
(*Source:* National Archives, U.S. Army Signal Corps.)

Port Moresby, Papua New Guinea, May 1944.

Women soldiers were quite a novelty to islanders. In this photograph, the first WACs (Women's Army Corps) to arrive in New Guinea are greeted by two Motuan men with gifts of *lakatoi,* sailing canoe models.
(*Source:* National Archives, U.S. Army Signal Corps.)

wages and prices. Economic controls, however, often proved impossible to enforce. Fixed wages were undercut every time a G.I. paid a child one dollar to climb a palm tree for a coconut. Even if wages were kept low, opportunities to work multiplied in the war economy.

A common opinion among Pacific islanders is that many in the military would have liked to pay workers more but were thwarted by colonial regulations. Workers from the Solomon Islands argue that some Americans told them, "We want to pay you like we pay ourselves, the same salaries. We want you to eat like we do because you do the same work that we do." Neli Lifuka, local head of the two hundred members of the labor corps on Funafuti, remembers similar American attitudes toward pay rates, contrasting with those of British authorities:

They [the British] didn't want the Americans to give us the wages they wanted to pay. We got seven dollars and fifty cents a month . . . I was the paymaster for all the natives . . . The American quartermaster told me about the trouble with the British. He showed me a paper which said that we should keep the money for us that was left over when I had paid the laborers but keep quiet about it (Koch 1978, 28).

Tongatapu, Tonga, September 1942.
Tongans sail out to the USS *Enterprise* to sell or trade beads, shells, grass skirts, and mats to the sailors.
(*Source:* National Archives, U.S. Navy.)

Tulagi, Solomon Islands, August 1943.
Islanders and sailors from the USS *Nicholas* exchange grass skirts for cigarettes. The grass skirt was unknown in many parts of the Pacific until the war.
(*Source:* National Archives, U.S. Navy.)

Many Pacific islanders became traders, bartering local produce and commodities for American and Japanese manufactured goods, or selling these products for dollars and yen. Regulations attempted to fix prices, as well as wages, in the canoes that pulled up alongside naval vessels, roadside stalls, bazaars, and marketplaces that grew up about military installations—such as the marketplace near the copra mill on Espiritu Santo, or the market that islanders established near ANGAU headquarters in Port Moresby. At some bases, authorities strove (futilely) to stop *all* trading. The New Hebrides Joint Regulation No. 1 of 1944 ordered: "The manufacture and sale of native curios (e.g. grass skirts, canoes, clubs, bracelets), except as authorised by the Resident Commissioners, is hereby prohibited." The regulation imposed a fine of up to fifty pounds and/or six months in prison for entrepreneurial island artisans.

In addition to 162 pounds of bananas, a U.S. dollar in wartime Tonga officially, at least, could buy 48 pounds of sweet corn, oranges, pineapples, or watermelon, 144 pounds of papaya, 84 pounds of sweet potatoes, or 24 pounds of peanuts (in the shell) (Weeks 1987, 425). In the Solomon Islands, officials attempted to set commodity prices at equally low rates. The price of four large or six small pumpkins was set at sixteen cents. Sixteen cents would also buy eight oranges, six large or twelve small pineapples, twelve small papayas, a dozen eggs, or thirty pounds of either sweet potatoes, yams, or taro. If a serviceman wanted to purchase six large or eight small watermelons, six grapefruit, or twelve large papayas he had to pay thirty-three cents. The price of a hen was set at sixty-six cents while roosters could be had for fifty cents each. Eight sugarcanes, on the other hand, officially were worth only eight cents, and a pound of fish went for a nickle.

In addition to garden produce, fowl, and seafood, islanders soon realized the market for curios and souvenirs—including selling Japanese money and equipment to the Americans and vice versa. Servicemen snapped up spears, bows and arrows, wooden turtles and other carvings, the ubiquitous grass skirt, circle pigs' tusks, seashells, baskets and mats, and model sailing canoes. The manufacture of walking sticks alone in the Solomon Islands must have been especially lucrative in that military authorities established a price schedule ranging from fifty cents for a cane made of "plain coconut wood" to

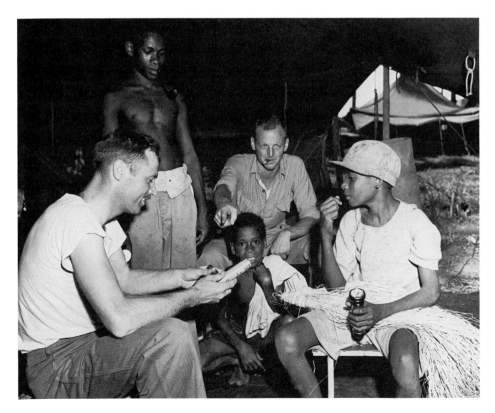

Guadalcanal, Solomon Islands, August 1943. Young traders offer money to buy a Marine's flashlight after he refused to swap it for two grass skirts. Jonathan Fifi'i, leader of a labor corps section on Guadalcanal, remembers the deep impression made by friendly relations with Americans. *"They invited us inside (their tents), and when we were inside, we could sit on their beds. We got inside and they gave us their glasses so we could drink out of them too. They gave us plates and we ate with their spoons. That was the first we had seen of that kind of thing. We talked about it like this, 'Those people like the British and the whites before, it was terrible because they were not kind to us! These people here are really nice to us. We can all sit on one bed, and we all eat together.'"* (*Source:* National Archives, U.S. Marine Corps.)

Guadalcanal, Solomon Islands, November 1943. Human skulls found a market during the war. In this photograph, an American corporal sells Japanese skulls and other souvenirs he has decorated with the Rising Sun. The photograph captures him and an islander swapping grass skirts for military clothing.
(*Source:* National Archives, U.S. Marine Corps.)

two dollars for one of dark ebony wood inlaid with mother-of-pearl shell. In the Solomons, some entrepreneurs found employment selling to servicemen "native curios" that actually were made by American Seabees. One observer noted, "It was not unusual to have a native make change for you from a roll of American bills an inch or more thick." The British, desperately attempting to gain control of this market, started an official trading post to deal in native crafts, "but the shop was a flop. The Seabees made better goods and sold them cheaper" (Chapman 1949, 77).

The war, in fact, in many parts of the Pacific was a formative influence on today's familiar "tourist arts" (Akin 1988). For the first time, islanders encountered large numbers of outsiders who were willing to pay for models or copies of traditional cultural artifacts. They also discovered a market for non-traditional objects (such as the "grass skirt" on many islands) that reflected existing American images of South Seas paradise isles. On those islands that had enjoyed a small trade in cultural curios before the war (such as Tonga), wartime demand inflated prices up to 400 percent of prewar values (Weeks 1987). The "airport art" that one encounters today around the world, in many cases, traces its antecedents to World War II marketplaces.

Most wartime dollars and yen eventually disappeared, sucked back into the surrounding Pacific rim economies. For example, using a fund amassed largely from the sale of mats and baskets to American servicemen, the people of Vaitupu, Tuvalu (formerly Ellice Islands) managed to purchase an island for resettlement near Fiji (Koch 1978, 45). More often, the dollars, the bartered or purchased cigarettes, wristwatches, and other wartime goods that islanders acquired from Allied and Japanese forces were used up, broken, or confiscated by returning colonial authorities attempting to reestablish the prewar status quo. Islanders today still complain of colonial agents taking away the money, uniforms, and other goods they had acquired as gifts or in trade from servicemen during the war (e.g., Counts 1989, 201). Nevertheless, those gifts given and received, those objects bartered or sold, still shine in people's memories. In many cases, more tangible reminders of the wartime exchange remain as well. Many an American visitor to Pacific villages today has had the experience of being shown a roll of U.S. coins, kept carefully wrapped, all with dates before 1945. Wartime acts of generosity and exchange for the first time extended traditional Pacific relations of giving and receiving beyond the horizon.

Sansapor, Irian Jaya (Dutch New Guinea), September or October 1944.
Islanders also found new markets for human skulls that were, in many areas, part of traditional religious practices. A trader poses behind a line of skulls with modeled faces he is offering for sale.
(*Source:* Anonymous.)

**Bougainville, Papua New
Guinea, May 1944.
Members of the Fijian Third
Battalion, dressed in traditional dance costume, honor
officers of the Allied forces
with a kava (*yaqona*) ceremony. Here a Fijian pours
the kava into an officer's cup
as cameras whir and click in
the background. Some weeks
earlier these Fijians had honored U.S. Major General
Griswold by presenting him
with a whale's tooth orna-
ment—a traditional sign of
chiefly status.**
(*Source:* National Archives,
U.S. Navy.)

9. Ceremony

Rituals and ceremonies are everywhere used to publicize and celebrate significant moments in social life. They are also highly photogenic. During occasions of public performance, cameras are focused upon enactments of ideals, identities, and relations that otherwise remain ambiguous or latent in everyday life. In the case of the war, ceremonies were organized to produce idealized portraits of islander loyalty and friendship, and so were a favored subject matter for photographers assigned the job of capturing images of loyal subjects and happy relations between military forces and local inhabitants.

As Allied and Japanese military personnel flooded into the islands to fight a war, they paused frequently to make public statements about their relations with the native population. By the same token, the people who watched their islands fill up with warring armies frequently sought to make their own statements about these relations, as *they* saw them. For islanders, these relations were more than a matter of individual acquaintance; they were also new or hoped-for group alliances. Traditional ceremonies, customarily used to express solidarity and collective identity, provided a means of incorporating the military newcomers within local frameworks of understanding.

As the parties to novel wartime encounters became more familiar with one another, they frequently expressed their newfound relations by inviting each other to participate in their own traditional practices, whether a dance, a welcoming ceremony, a flag raising, or a football game. With the construction of new buildings, bridges, and the like at military bases, dedication ceremonies could now incorporate "native" singing and dancing as embellishments to the usual forms of speechmaking and entertainment. Joint participation could be a way of demonstrating new alliances, or of acknowledging respect for the other's cultural heritage. It could also be a way of having fun.

Custom

Villages were frequently off limits to military personnel. When servicemen and -women *did* visit local villages, however, it was usually for special events offering hospitality and gifts as tokens of goodwill. In island communities, relations with one's neighbors, allies, and in-laws are affirmed by feasts to which they are invited as honored guests and feted with food, gifts, and entertainment. When military newcomers were invited to feasts, villagers who were spectators of the war became principal performers, and the combatants became the audience. These occasions were an opportunity for islanders to display their traditions and sometimes to instruct servicemen in local ways. Arthur Dana of Buna, Papua New Guinea, recalls how the Australian captain of the Papuan Infantry Battalion came to his area near the end of the war for a big celebration: "All the people were putting on traditional dances. He arrived with many white girls. They arrived to watch the dances. It was in the night and the moonlight was very bright . . . bombers from Rabaul later ruined the party."

St. Louis Village, New Caledonia, July 1942.
Two American nurses join in a "native" dance to the amusement of all concerned. The dance was part of festivities put on by villagers to entertain members of the Americal Division. The original photo caption reads, "The natives are very fond of American soldiers and have relaxed many a tribal taboo for their entertainment."
(*Source:* National Archives, U.S. Army Signal Corps.)

Ngatpang, Palau, October(?) 1945.
Just after the end of the war, Palauan children pay a consolation visit to Japanese military confined at their former headquarters. Here they entertain with traditional dances. Note that the boys are wearing Japanese caps. (*Source:* Yoshiyasu Morikawa.)

All over the Pacific, military delegations were welcomed ashore with mock attacks, elaborate handshaking or hymn-singing, feasted with sumptuous amounts of food, presented with gifts, and entertained with dancing and singing on into the night. Michael Somare remembers that his people in the Murik area of Papua New Guinea used to dance for the occupying Japanese forces and they, in turn, would perform sword dances for the villagers (Somare 1970, 32).

The renown of an island feast or ceremony is gauged by the importance of those who attend as guests. Military officers and servicemen were potential guests who could greatly elevate the prestige of village ceremonies. In one such instance, several high-ranking officers of the American forces on Guadalcanal accepted an invitation to attend the final, public day of an elaborate initiation ceremony staged by the people of Santa Ana in 1943 (Mead 1973). The Americans (who brought their own photographer) arrived in style in a flying-boat and subchaser. Brought ashore in canoes, they were greeted with a war dance and mock challenge by spear-waving "warriors." They were then walked through the village and seated in a temporary feast house and presented with decorated carved bowls of food. The villagers put on a mimed skit for the entertainment of their American guests, depicting their "enslavement" by Japanese conquerors.

In societies such as Fiji, Samoa, and Tonga, ritual forms traditionally employed to mark the status of high chiefs were extended to demonstrate local regard for important military officers. When a U.S. naval hospital was completed in Samoa, the dedication service consisted of a kava ceremony followed by a feast. With twenty-five Samoans sitting along one wall of the house, and twenty-five American officers sitting along the other, both Samoans and Americans made speeches, and at least one of the Americans re-

Suva, Fiji, February 1944.
Three Fijian police get a first-hand look at an American tradition transported to the Pacific: the Army-Navy football game. Here they pose with three sailors, complete with U.S. Navy flag and mascot, at Albert Park in Suva, site of the 1944 game.
(*Source:* National Archives, U.S. Army Signal Corps.)

Tutuila, American Samoa, 1942.
A commanding officer swears four Samoans into the U.S. Marine Corps. Because of the need for manpower, the Marine Corps was opened up to Samoan recruitment for the first time during the early months of World War II. Such swearing-in ceremonies marked the young men's passage into their newfound military status.
(*Source:* National Archives, U.S. Marine Corps.)

New Georgia, Solomon
Islands, October 1943.
Sgt. Andrew Langabaea of
the Solomon Islands Defence
Force marches across the pa-
rade ground with eight U.S.
officers to receive the Purple
Heart for wounds received
during the fighting for New
Georgia.
(*Source:* National Archives,
U.S. Army Signal Corps.)

ceived a chiefly title. Everyone was served kava according to a customary order of precedence, with the ranking Navy doctor, as host, receiving the traditional last drink (Parsons 1945, 136–37).

In these and other Pacific societies where hierarchical leadership status is marked by ritual gifts and decorations, military officers were often presented with objects such as whale's teeth, shell necklaces, and decorated walking sticks, to signify their "chiefly" stature. For example, U.S. Maj. Gen. R. B. Lincoln received a floral tribute from Chief Nate Kaoum of the island of Voh in New Caledonia, making him an "honorary chief."

Patriotism

Whereas villagers engaged in feasting, dancing, and other ceremonial practices, the Allies and Japan also used ritual and ceremony to celebrate nationalism, patriotism, and militarism. Those islanders who were members of defense forces took part in military ceremonies that marked their entry into and out of those units, signifying their allegiance to one or another of the warring powers. Acts of islander sacrifice and bravery were also singled out for ceremonial recognition by awards of military decorations, providing occasions to restate ideals of loyalty and sacrifice.

For the warring armies, the most potent customs and ceremonies were those that celebrated the nations and cultures for which they were fighting. Both the Allies and Japanese engaged islanders in their national ceremonies. Liberation was marked by flag raisings, bravery by the award of medals, and loyalty rewarded with gifts and patriotic speeches. And all of this was accompanied by small but significant rituals of bowing, marching and drilling, sa-

Salamaua, Papua New Guinea, September 1943. Papua New Guinean police stand at attention for a flag-raising ceremony to mark the recapture of the Salamaua area. A European missionary resident in the area had taken the flag down prior to the Japanese occupation the previous year, and it is here "put back in its original place by his hand."
(*Source:* National Archives, U.S. Army Signal Corps.)

luting, and singing national anthems. For example, the May 1945 issue of the *Pacific Islands Monthly* noted that the chief of a New Caledonian tribe staged a feast at which exservicemen from World War I were awarded decorations to the accompaniment of patriotic speeches. In another instance, the residents of Majuro, Marshall Islands, were collectively given a commendation by U.S. forces in January 1945 for their attempt to rescue two Marine aviators downed near their atoll.

The Japanese in Palau exhorted the local populace to gather every morning at designated workplaces for organized ceremonies, including patriotic speeches by the labor bosses, singing the Japanese national anthem, and worshipping toward the emperor's palace in Tokyo (Higuchi 1986, 31). In addition, an oath to the emperor was repeated each morning:

> We are the children of the Emperor.
> We shall become splendid Japanese.
> We shall be loyal to Japan.

Fais, Federated States of Micronesia, January 1945. Fais Islanders try out a new custom: saluting the American flag. Villagers gather for a ceremonial occasion marking the end of thirty years of Japanese rule, and the beginning of the American era. A flagpole erected in front of the island's men's house provides the appropriate prop for symbolizing new loyalties.
(*Source:* National Archives, U.S. Navy.)

Majuro, Marshall Islands, July 4, 1944.
Quick to become attuned to the American ritual calendar, hundreds of Marshallese staged an elaborate ceremony to celebrate American independence and, according to the wartime caption, "their own recent freedom from the Japanese." The event consisted of singing and dancing as well as the presentation of gifts to the U.S. commander on Majuro, shown receiving shell necklaces from local women.
(*Source:* National Archives, U.S. Marine Corps.)

As U.S. forces occupied Micronesia, the Americans replaced these Japanese rituals with some of their own, especially flag raisings accompanied by the U.S. Pledge of Allegiance.

Islanders reciprocated in kind by organizing their own ceremonies during which they presented military forces with food, gifts, and other tokens of their regard for their powerful new allies. Islanders frequently incorporated elements of the foreigners' own traditions in the events they sponsored. On July 4, 1944, hundreds of Marshallese staged an elaborate ceremony honoring the American independence day. One photo shows the U.S. naval commander in the area seated beneath a huge flag receiving gifts of rare shells. Christian ceremonies were also an important idiom for expressions of bonds between islanders and military groups. In Guadalcanal, Vella Lavella, and Nissan (Green) Island, islanders built the most splendid churches they had ever constructed and presented these to Allied forces (see chapter 11). The dedication of a new Catholic church on the coast of Guadalcanal also became an occasion for inviting American military brass for a grand celebration, island style. Fr. Emery de Klerk described the event in his diary:

Chaplain Schneider and Doctor Johnson arrive by Cub. Admiral Gunther and Commander Wagner by seaplane. New Zealand Catalina brings beer supplies plus New Zealand and American flags. Afternoon: Arrival Commander Lees (CO Henderson Field) and Chaplain Mayberry. Shortly afterward arrival of Major General Shepherd and Colonel Mcgaien. Little odds and ends of majors and captains. . . .

Guadalcanal, Solomon Islands, January 1944. On behalf of Solomon Islanders, Jacob Vouza of the Solomon Islands Defence Force, an honorary sergeant major in the U.S. Marine Corps, presents a plaque of gratitude to the commander of U.S. forces on the island. The wooden plaque is inscribed, "To the United States Navy, with appreciation from the people of the British Solomon Islands, Guadalcanal, 1944." (*Source:* National Archives, U.S. Navy.)

Over seven hundred natives are present. Solemn High Mass. Over 400 Communions. After church official dances till 11:00 o'clock when Admiral Gunther has to leave. When the Admiral leaves the beach all the natives gather and give him three war whoops [British cheers]. They resume dances until 2 P.M. when General Sheppard has to leave. Then starts division of 25 pigs and 5 cows. Brig. Gen. Clement arrives at five. Fri. and Sat. ferry guests across the mountains to Lunga.

Although larger than most village celebrations, the ceremony to dedicate the Tangarare Catholic church was typical of many occasions in which villagers worked to incorporate military newcomers into their lives. When the exigencies of war permitted, islanders organized ceremonies to make important officers into "chiefs," to recognize military and national powers as allies, and to acknowledge a common humanity that was often denied in the context of prewar colonial life. For their part, both Allied and Japanese military forces also ceremonially enacted their versions of relations with Pacific islanders—whether inducting them into service roles, certifying allegiance, or applauding heroism. Throughout, film cameras rolled and shutters clicked as ceremonial activities sought to evoke desired wartime realities.

Guadalcanal, Solomon Islands, October 1944.
The war spread new musical styles and instruments across the Pacific. An American Marine directs a band of "native swingsters," the "Jungle Rhythm Boys," as they practice in preparation for a dance. The photograph's original caption points out that in the background "a couple of jitterbugs can't resist the rhythm [and] begin to dance." (*Source:* National Archives, U.S. Marine Corps.)

10. Music

A Marine observer on Efate wrote, "I shall never forget one morning's sight of a native gang tramping to work to the harmonized chant of 'God Bless America.' The strains echoed feelingly through the jungle long after they had passed. Another favorite was 'The Marine's Hymn.' This became a tribal favorite, although many natives still had to learn just what a Marine was" (Heinl 1944, 240). If islanders were singing American military and patriotic tunes in Vanuatu, the songs heard across Micronesia, the Admiralty Islands, Bougainville, and the northern coast of New Guinea were in Japanese. Many Papua New Guineans still recall the Japanese anthems they learned to sing at schools the Japanese established for local children (Somare 1970; 1975).

Pacific island cultures have rich musical traditions onto which a number of imported styles have been layered. Christian missionaries, traders, settlers, and administrators all brought various kinds of music along with them into the Pacific. Before the war, many islanders were members of Christian choirs and could sing large repertoires of hymns. Others performed in military bands, such as those of Guam and Samoa. Many learned popular Western songs. Prewar favorites such as "Show Me the Way to Go Home," and "God Be with You 'til We Meet Again" were sung throughout the Pacific. In Hawaii, local musicians developed musical styles that continue to influence modern Pacific music today. Many islanders were expert musical performers. When Marines landed at Buma Mission, Malaita, for example, a local fourteen-year-old boy (with a guitar given him by a navy chief) entertained them with perhaps the most widely known American song at that time, "You Are My Sunshine."

Life on isolated Pacific bases was often routine and boring. Local musicians discovered a friendly audience for their talents. Allied and Japanese servicemen listened to at least a sample of indigenous musical styles at performances and ceremonies when island dance teams entertained military personnel. Work gangs in Vanuatu would often enliven long days or nights of unloading cargo with impromptu dance performances on ships' decks. Occasionally, however, the war hindered traditional musical performance. The Japanese in New Guinea banned the playing of slit gongs, fearing that drumming could transmit messages about troop movements. They broke up people's skin drums in the Buna area for the same reason.

Wartime photographs record numerous musical performances across the Pacific. In the Solomon Islands, singers from the Fijian Infantry Brigade were popular performers. Recordings of their war era songs still find a ready market in Fiji today. Solomon Islands bands and choirs performed for American troops as well. Their music was sometimes an island version of 1940s swing,

Port Moresby(?), Papua New Guinea, March 1944. Traditional musical styles join with the new. A young bugler from the Royal Papuan Constabulary Band, established in 1943, plays alongside a team of traditional *kundu* drummers. The photo's release exaggerates: "The band was started 6 months ago, none of the selected natives knowing a note of music."
(*Source:* Australian War Memorial.)

sometimes a rendition of Christmas hymns. And on Guam, one photograph captures three young children singing "Pistol Packin' Mama" into a Marine microphone.

The establishment of sophisticated communication systems at island bases brought Pacific music into the modern era. During the war, local musicians were broadcast on radio, in most cases for the first time. In addition to the "Singing Cruz Brothers" on Guam, radio carried the tunes of many other island performers to large audiences. Radio Munda's regular Sunday afternoon program featured a choir composed of members of the Solomon Islands Defence Force. Marines taped a Christmas program on December 25, 1943, that included a local choir from Miravari, Vella Lavella, singing hymns. Five miles of telephone wire were laid in order that the service might be available for local broadcasting as well as subsequent rebroadcasting in America. Islanders encountered other new musical technology during the war, including phonographs and tape-recorders.

The convulsions of battle—troop concentrations, population movements, and new musical technologies—shook up once insular musical traditions. Instruments such as the harmonica, guitar, ukulele, and electric organ became more widely used. New musical styles were heard. Chief Kalosike of North Efate, for example, learned to play the harmonica from American servicemen and, decades later, still could play "Pretty Baby." Elder Johnson Nase of Tanna recalls learning to play the guitar from a Samoan he met during the war. Nase became one of the first skilled guitar players in southern Vanuatu.

Lautoka, Fiji, February 1944. Members of Fiji's Second Battalion Labour Corps sing over a bowl of kava. Fijian singers were popular performers at Allied entertainments.
(*Source:* Fiji Ministry of Information.)

**Guam, January 1945.
Pedro, Ricardo, and Jose
Cruz entertain the Marines
with their version of "Pistol
Packin' Mama."**
(*Source:* National Archives,
U.S. Marine Corps.)

Clement Felo of Santa Isabel still plays and sings the English lyrics to an entire repertoire of country-western songs he learned from American friends while working in the labor corps as a young boy. On at least one occasion Felo performed those and other songs as part of a USO Christmas show for American troops in the Russell Islands.

New songs found their way into the region, carried by ordinary servicemen humming and singing as they worked, or carried by radio, recordplayer, and tape-recorder. Cinema, stage plays, and USO shows also brought new music to islander ears. Photographs, for example, capture composer Irving Berlin's encounters with an island audience. The war's musical influences contributed to the development of today's "string band" and to other contemporary Pacific musical and performance styles.

In addition to learning English or Japanese songs and developing skills on the guitar, ukulele, and gut bucket, islanders everywhere composed their own new songs about wartime experiences and encounters. In societies without writing, songs serve as important archives, or data banks, of historical events. Islanders regularly compose songs to record significant happenings in their communities. People often commission a song from a local composer in order to commemorate a special feast or ceremony. The events of the war—sometimes exciting, sometimes deadly—provided obvious material for island composers. On Kolombangara, for example, people today sing about "Captain Kennedy and the PT-109." War songs encapsulate local historical understandings of the war. Some tell of the occupation of homelands by for-

Munda, New Georgia, Solomon Islands, August 1944. Bill Gina, David Hoto (guitar), and other singers from the Solomon Islands Defense Force perform on the military's Radio Munda—a regular Sunday afternoon feature.
(*Source:* National Archives, U.S. Army Signal Corps.)

Guadalcanal, Solomon Islands, August 1943. In addition to radio, the war brought other new musical technologies into the Pacific. Two Solomon Islanders spin records with an American GI. (*Source:* National Archives, U.S. Army Signal Corps.)

eign armies, and of resistance to the Japanese or American invaders. Some record the terrors of battle, and the power and cargo of the combatants. Some celebrate the work that islanders performed in either Allied or Japanese labor corps. Others lament the deaths of loved ones, and the destruction of villages and gardens.

Some of these new war songs became famous across the region. The Fijian Infantry Brigade's rendition of "Isolei" is a popular standard even today. "Raisi Mo" ("More Rice" or "Only Rice")—a song lamenting the monotonous diet of ANGAU laborers—is well known in Papua New Guinea. A popular song from the Solomon Islands, "Kaikai Popo" ("Eating Pawpaw"), similarly records the war's restrictive effects on local diet. Other popular war songs from the Solomon Islands include "Wakabaot Long Saenataon Ia" ("Walking around Chinatown"), and the widely renowned "Ha Ha Japani Ha Ha."

These songs continue to remind older islanders of their war experiences. They also transmit an understanding of the war to children and grandchildren born after the Japanese surrender. Many are songs of remembrance. These record the partings of islanders from the new friends they made during the war years. One song of goodbye from Sikaiana, for example, laments the departure of American flyers who had crash-landed on the lagoon (Donner 1989, 154):

> America your plane circles the island
> When it turn to go, my heart swoons
> When they walk to climb into the plane I cry
> We have not yet said goodbye.

**Ulithi, Federated States of
Micronesia, January 1945.
An American Catholic priest,
standing next to a makeshift
altar set up on the beach to
give a prayer service, presents a young Micronesian
girl with a rosary.**
(*Source:* National Archives,
U.S. Navy.)

11. Religion

The momentous, mysterious, and dangerous events of World War II were ultimately explained by Pacific islanders in religious terms, whether traditional or Christian. Islanders drew upon beliefs about ancestor spirits and mythic heroes as well as about the Christian God to make sense of the events that descended upon them during the war. Furthermore, they actively used ritual practices of all kinds (from prayer to magic and sorcery) to protect themselves, help their allies, and attack their enemies.

Christianity

In the small islands and coastal regions where most of the Pacific War was fought, local residents had a long history of contact with outsiders. The hundreds of thousands of newcomers who came into the region for the first time during the war frequently expressed surprise at local people's sophistication with Western ways.

Perhaps more than any other aspect of island culture, the widespread practice of Christianity may have most violated the preconceptions of servicemen who expected to find primitive "natives" or ferocious cannibals. Although the missions in many areas suffered badly from Japanese occupation, they also benefited from the attention the war focused on their once remote outposts. Christianity was often mentioned as a major factor in the transformation of Papua New Guineans into their wartime image as humane "fuzzy wuzzy angels" saving Australian lives. Even as the war raged, two books were published that chronicled the contributions of missions and island Christians to the war effort (Henrich 1944; Van Dusen 1945). As one begins: "'Dear Mom: Because of the missions, I was feasted and not feasted upon when I fell from

Cape Gloucester, New Britain, Papua New Guinea, March 1944.
The American landings on Cape Gloucester made it possible for people of the area to reactivate their practice of Christianity. Here a U.S. Navy priest hands out rosaries.
(*Source:* National Archives, U.S. Marine Corps.)

Cape Gloucester, New Britain, Papua New Guinea, March 1944.
The first Christian service is held on Cape Gloucester since the Japanese imprisoned the resident missionary priest two years previously. Even though the church building had been torn down, and some people appeared out of practice, the priest found that "the communicants knew their responses better than American Catholics."
(*Source:* National Archives, U.S. Marine Corps.)

the sky into this village.' Through such homespun comments in their V-mail, many an American family is awakening to the fact that unexpected discoveries beyond coral atolls and foxholes, jungles and Japanese are being made by their boys in far places" (Van Dusen 1945, xi).

This book goes on to report many such "discoveries" of competent, educated Christian islanders by military newcomers. In one instance, an American commander remarking on the experience of a patrol led by Solomon Islanders comments, "The great shock of [the] 'wilderness expedition' was when the natives used to motion them to sit down at about 6 A.M. and 6 P.M. every day, pull out a book and start conducting religious ceremonies . . . one of the favorite tunes was clearly 'Onward Christian Soldiers'!" (ibid., 32).

For those islanders who practiced it, Christianity was often the single greatest symbol of a common bond with the Allies. Both islanders and Allied soldiers possessed knowledge of Christian ritual practices such as praying, singing hymns, and attending church services and funerals. By jointly engaging in these activities, they demonstrated a degree of shared culture meaningful to both parties. One American soldier wrote home that he had come upon a local work group constructing a house with one man perched on top, "singing the hymn 'Jesus Christ is risen today' in his own native tongue. It was at first quite a shock to me but I realized that he had learnt it from the missionary . . . He came down from his perch and began to sing again. I listened then joined him in English. How strange it was to hear this primitive boy and myself singing praises to *our* God" (Henrich 1944, 42).

Allied chaplains regularly conducted church services and administered communion to islanders, whether in their villages or on military bases. For their part, island catechists and priests assisted in these services and, on some occasions, organized their own ceremonies. For example, the dedication of a new naval hospital in Samoa was marked by a kava ceremony that involved extensive speechmaking by Samoan chiefs who found meaning and purpose for the event in Christianity and in the long history of Christian activity in the islands. The first chief to speak "stood and asked God's blessing on the house, prayed for continued friendship between Americans and [Samoans] and thanked God for sending the Americans to [Samoa] and the hospital to [Pago Pago]" (Parsons 1945, 135).

On Guadalcanal, Vella Lavella, and Nissan, islanders also built elaborately constructed churches at the site of Allied cemeteries, and presented them to Allied troops with ceremonial expressions of gratitude. The memorial chapel erected at the heart of the American military cemetery on Guadalcanal where sixteen hundred men were buried is a particularly good example (Van Dusen 1945, 44–45). Built entirely of local materials and labor, the Guadalcanal church was, according to some observers, "the finest known example of Solomon Island artistry and craftsmanship" (ibid., 44). It was constructed in the shape of a cross, with a belltower rising above the thatched roof. The dedication ceremony, held on September 12, 1943, was an occasion for Solomon Islanders to ceremonially present it to the Americans, with a British

Dumpu, Papua New Guinea, October 1943.
Corporal Raka of the Papuan Infantry Battalion and Sergeant Guy of the 21st Australian Infantry Brigade share a hymn sheet at a "church parade" in the Ramu Valley.
(*Source:* Australian War Memorial.)

officer acting as intermediary. Three speeches were given: "Native to British Officer," "British to American People," and "Acceptance for United States." The spokesman for the Solomon Islanders is quoted as having said, "We want to thank the Americans and Allies who have fought to push the enemy out of our land. Now we give this church to you. But this church [does not] belong to you and me. This church belongs to God." Following the dedication ceremony, "Onward Christian Soldiers" and the last verse of "America" were sung by all.

Religious exchanges also moved in the other direction, from Allied military to islanders. Thirty men of the U.S. 40th Army Division assisted Fr. Emery de Klerk and his flock to rebuild their church at their mission station at Tangarare on Guadalcanal. The church was later dedicated on November 29, 1944, in an elaborate ceremony attended by numerous U.S. servicemen and over seven hundred islanders (see chapter 9).

Again and again throughout the Pacific, narrow escapes from death or injury were explained in terms of divine protection. In the village of Kia on Santa Isabel, an American bomb went through the roof of the church—the most imposing building in the village—but remained unexploded until defused at the end of the war. Peter Taloni of Malaita gives testimony echoed by many islanders: "Several weeks later we went back to our village and saw those bombs which lay around and inside the village. Nothing else was destroyed in our village. From what had happened I began to realize that there was something great which God had done for us. So then I became a good Christian" (Keeble 1980, 8).

Just as Christianity provided an important bond with Allied troops, it was often a barrier to acceptance of the Japanese. In some Christian strongholds, Japanese occupiers provoked strong resentment by mistreating missionaries and desecrating churches. On strongly Catholic Guam, the Chamorro population saw their cathedral turned into a jail to confine captured Americans, and then into an entertainment center where islanders were called upon to perform traditional dances (Palomo 1984, 83).

Guadalcanal, Solomon Islands, April 1944. Members of the Solomon Islands Labour Corps recruited from the island of Malaita receive communion together with American servicemen as part of an outdoor Easter service.
(*Source:* National Archives, U.S. Navy.)

Vangunu, Solomon Islands, December 1943.
A resident Tongan missionary, Paul Harvea, leads a Solomon Islands choir in singing hymns during church services held for American military based in the New Georgia area.
(*Source:* National Archives, U.S. Navy.)

Even in occupied areas where the Japanese tolerated Christianity, the evacuation, imprisonment, or execution of most Western missionaries effectively suppressed its practice. By the end of the war, about two hundred foreign missionaries had died in Papua New Guinea alone (Nelson 1982, 198). People who had evacuated coastal villages found themselves without priest or church, and thus without the spiritual protection and strength they sought through Christianity. A major part of liberation for many peoples in Japanese-occupied islands was the renewal of Christian ritual life. In Cape Gloucester, New Britain, two village catechists who had hidden their church chalices in the forest brought them out for the first church service in two years after Allied troops retook the area.

The Japanese did not often actively promote Shinto religion as a replacement for Christianity or traditional practices. On Palau, however, where they had thirty years of involvement with the local populace, the approach of war spurred the construction of an important shrine that, for the first time, was opened up for use by Palauans as well as by Japanese (Higuchi 1986). Although twenty-four shrines had been built by Japanese settlers in Micronesia prior to 1940, only Japanese people visited them for worship. When the new shrine was built by the government, Palauans were urged to worship as well, in order to pray for national victory in war and for soldiers' success. This joint worship of Japanese and Palauans signified a new solidarity between islander and outsider, just as Christian services did elsewhere in the Pacific.

Traditional Religion

When faced with the incredible dangers and uncertainties of World War II, Pacific islanders also protected themselves with traditional ritual practices. These typically involved calling upon powerful spirits for assistance, usually the spirits of deceased ancestors. Inhabitants of the Micronesian atoll of Lamotrek composed the following song, lauding the power of their ancestral spirits to protect them from the destructive effects of American and Japanese bombings:

> The people cannot sleep because they are afraid that the American planes
>   will drop bombs;
> They are crying but at the same time they are pleased with the spirits
> because the spirits are standing in the middle of the ocean and watching for
>   enemy ships and planes;
> The spirits guard the southern part of Lamotrek
> and if American planes come the spirits go into the planes and sit with the
>   pilots;
> When pilots make a decision to drop a bomb,
> the spirits make sure that it is dropped in a place that won't kill any people;
> Those spirits also said that they will destroy Japanese planes
> by pulling out screws in the planes' engines.

Even where people drew upon Christian ritual and belief for support, traditional magic and sorcery were often employed as well to supplement the arsenal of spiritual defense.

Prior to pacification, warfare had been a special focus for religious ritual in many island cultures. Spirits were consulted both before and after raiding expeditions. In some cases, enemy captives became human sacrifices offered up to ancestral spirits to ensure their continued benevolence. Charles Fox, a longtime missionary in the Solomon Islands, reported the resurgence of this ancient custom following a U.S. Marine raid on a Japanese radio outpost on the island of Malaita: "About five hundred heathen hillmen were at the back of the Americans and rushed in to collect the blood of the dead and dying Japanese to sacrifice to the spirits . . . That day I met parties of excited natives running along wearing the clothes of the dead Japanese. They were seeing how white men wage war" (Fox 1962, 124).

Islanders in many areas used war magic and hunting magic in dangerous situations. Many who were recruited into military units tell of relying upon

Vella Lavella, Solomon Islands, January 1944. People of Vella Lavella join in ceremonies to dedicate a "memorial chapel" they built for American and New Zealand military forces fighting in the area. The chapel stands at the site of an Allied cemetery. The roofridge of this finely constructed building is decorated with bird figures made from the roots of coconut palms.
(*Source:* National Archives, U.S. Marine Corps.)

magic to avoid detection and injury in battle. By chanting the proper words or employing the appropriate ingredients, one might disorient the enemy and cause his bullets to miss the mark. For example, a sergeant major of the Papuan Infantry Battalion tells in the movie *Angels of War* of his use of magical ash to save his men from Japanese bullets: "If you follow these instructions, your bullets will enter the bodies of the enemy, but the enemy bullets will not touch you . . . This power came down from my ancestors and it was passed on to me. I gave this power to the soldiers under my command. We have defeated the enemy through these customs and no other."

In another example where ancestor spirits provided protection from World War II bullets, a Solomon Islander who helped evacuate a group of nuns by paddling them across the open sea claims that they were saved by a traditional priest who uttered a spell to make them invisible to Japanese planes overhead. Many island cultures found new uses for traditional sorcery practices designed to attack enemies. Most Americans fighting in the Solomons were probably not aware that they had new allies on Ambrym in Vanuatu, where sorcerers were helping their friends by directing spirit attacks against the Japanese (Gwero 1988).

In parts of Papua New Guinea, people attributed Japanese successes over the Australians to Japanese use of magic and sorcery. Some people who saw the Japanese for the first time speculated that they might be the returned spirits of dead ancestors (Somare 1970). In fact, in the years preceding the war, Japanese newspapers had run articles about New Guinea cargo cults, so when they landed in 1942, some may have presented themselves as messen-

Lunga, Guadalcanal, Solomon Islands, September 1943. Members of the Solomon Islands Labour Corps and Allied servicemen dedicate a memorial chapel constructed by the laborers as a gift for the United States forces. The chapel was situated at the heart of the military cemetery on Guadalcanal where 1,600 Americans were buried. Built by several thousand islanders in just two months, the chapel had a seating capacity of 280.
(*Source:* National Archives, U.S. Marine Corps.)

gers sent by the ancestors (Gesch 1985). After all, they were obviously powerful enough to have forced a quick European evacuation.

Attempts at explaining the war's bewildering events sometimes gave rise to cults aimed at attaining new forms of power and wealth unattainable in the prewar colonial world. Where cult prophets overtly challenged Allied or Japanese authority they encountered a harsh and punitive response. For example, the Australians executed nine leaders of an antiwhite cult near Vanatinai (then Sudest Island) for their role in the murder of a district officer who was attempting to reestablish colonial control at the end of 1942 (Lepowsky 1989). The Japanese beheaded three cult leaders in Buka, and also killed hundreds of cultists in Irian Jaya (Worsley 1968).

Given that religion pervades most aspects of life in traditional Pacific societies, and that Christian missions had already established themselves in most of the areas where Allied and Japanese military forces set up their bases, it was inevitable that islanders would use religion to explain and cope with the war's effects. Both islanders and servicemen drew upon religious symbols to communicate common identity and purpose. In some cases, as in Guam, religion also became an idiom of difference and defiance, further exacerbating troubled relations between occupiers and an indigenous population. More often, however, religious practices—primarily those of Christianity—provided a language for making statements about shared goals and values that could be counterposed to the obvious disparities that otherwise separated the technologically sophisticated newcomers from Pacific villagers.

Guadalcanal, Solomon Islands, January 1944. Both islanders and servicemen had strong images of what each other should look like. Military photographers sometimes played with the distance between image and reality, as in the caption Capt. Donald L. Kettler wrote for this shot of Cpl. Luigi J. Greasso: "Bedecked with five-and-ten jewelry, grass skirt, walking cane and with a nickel cigar in his mouth, this Marine artilleryman shows the natives of this South Pacific island what a Hollywood native looks like. The natives were highly impressed; the rumor now is that there will be revolutionary change in dresses [*sic*] styles on the Solomon Island [*sic*]."
(*Source:* National Archives, U.S. Marine Corps.)

12. Conclusion: Images

When the millions of Allied troops who passed through the Pacific Theater first arrived on palm-bedecked islands, most had distinct ideas about what the islanders who lived there ought to be like. Their expectations were fed by travelers' tales of the South Seas and Hollywood films, such as the 1930s *Mutiny on the Bounty,* in which the rigors of shipboard life were traded for the sensuous pleasures of Polynesia. Dorothy Lamour's films, such as *The Jungle Princess* (1936) and *Her Jungle Love* (1938), especially shaped these expectations.

Prewar Western musings about the Pacific islands had depicted islanders in such discrepant terms as fierce cannibals on the one hand, and amorous maidens on the other. Not surprisingly, these stereotypic images, particularly those of beautiful women eager to consort with white-skinned strangers, were often found to be out of line with reality. In a sardonic novel about a naval outpost in Micronesia, the discrepancy between American stereotypes and island realities turns the first encounter between American troops and islanders into a farce:

The landing craft roared in over the green and lucid shallows . . . The door dropped and the sergeant led his men forward in a stumbling rush . . . They dropped on the sandward side of the logs. Behind them other men carried the tripod of a 50 calibre machine gun . . . Nothing stirred. Rucinski said: "Jeez! The air boys was right. No Japs! . . . Where's Dorothy Lamour?" [a native appears on the beach:] "It's a nigger, sergeant. Shall I let him have it? . . . The brown figure was coming towards them slowly . . . His hand swept over his mouth, and he said slowly, pulling out the syllables, "Guten Morgen." "Christ!" said Rucinski. "No Dorothy Lamour, and a nigger that speaks German!" (Divine 1950, 67–68).

When so disappointed, military men sometimes constructed their own images of the stereotypic native in order to authenticate their sojourn into the

173

Mok Island, Papua New Guinea, March 1944. Islanders and servicemen acted out their images of the other by cross-dressing. Islanders put on military uniforms; and GIs dressed like natives. Returning from Mok Island, the crew of Motor Transport Battalion 324 poses for a photograph dressed up in the beads and loincloths they obtained in exchange for cigarettes, razor blades, and odd bits of cloth. (*Source:* National Archives, U.S. Army Signal Corps.)

South Seas as they imagined this *should* be. On March 28, 1944, the entire crew of Motor Transport Battalion 324 dressed themselves in beads, arm bands, and loincloths they had acquired on Mok Island in exchange for razor blades, cigarettes, and "odd bits of cloth." (Mok is near Manus in the Admiralties.) Posing as natives, they sat for a group photograph. Captured on film, such incidents of "cross-dressing"—Americans dressed as islanders, and islanders dressed as soldiers and sailors—give a picture of the images each had of the other. We can see in action here ideas of self in relation to outsiders, to "others." Who are we? And who are they?

Prewar Pacific islanders had certain understandings of Europeans, Americans, Japanese, and other outsiders, just as Americans, for their part, entertained notions of South Seas "natives." The personal encounters, interactions, and events of the war had important consequences for these images. Expectations about the other became unsettled. More significantly, as conceptions of the other changed and deepened on both sides, so did understandings of the place of the self and one's own society in the postwar world.

Islanders represented their changing images of self and other in songs, stories, and—occasionally—in pictorial form. Few, if any, Pacific islanders owned cameras. They did, however, picture their wartime encounters by means of traditional media of representation. Expert weavers, island women incorporated U.S. flags and other military themes into the designs of their mats. On Malaita, in the Solomon Islands, one artisan replaced the frigate bird motif on large crescent-shaped pendants with an American eagle. In Japanese Micronesia, the rising sun appeared in tattoos. On Palau where there is a long tradition of carving "storyboards"—planks of wood that decorate men's houses with representations of historical events—World War II scenes were soon incorporated in these carvings. One set of war-era storyboards pictures Palauans hard at work for the Japanese as a fleet of American bombers circles overhead.

In many parts of the Pacific, islanders also represented their images of the war in small dramas or skits. Lauro villagers from Choiseul Island, for example, celebrated the Japanese withdrawal from their island with a feast and a tableau. In this, three islanders, dressed in Japanese uniforms, were stalked by local island scouts:

At a given signal they all opened fire [with blank rounds provided by a coastwatcher] and the enemy trio gave a most realistic display of the convulsive actions of dying Nips. Then followed a rush for the loot, which of course always actually happened,

Saipan, Northern Mariana Islands, Spring 1942. Japanese troops also dressed up as islanders. Posing in a studio complete with painted backdrop and three islanders, sailors of the Japanese navy's Fifth Communication Troop dressed in local fashion for a sports meeting at which they also sang and danced a traditional Saipan song.
(*Source:* Kyuya Takenaka.)

Butibum, Papua New Guinea, November 1944. Images of the South Seas influenced the taking of pictures during the war. Military photographers posed islanders according to notions of what natives are like. An Australian military filmmaker poses refugees from the Japanese occupation who have been resettled near Lae by ANGAU.
(*Source:* Australian War Memorial.)

and to the huge delight of the assembled multitude especially the Lauro ladies, they pulled every stitch of clothes off one bloke, who had to grab a banana leaf (Rhoades 1982, 54).

In another skit, also performed for Allied guests, Solomon Islanders on Santa Ana mimicked the harsh conditions endured during the Japanese occupation by showing an old, emaciated villager being pulled along on a rope by a Japanese military officer (depicted with a life-sized carved manikin). In these dramatic events villagers replayed war images and themes they shared with their victorious Western allies.

If islanders represented the war in their skits, weavings, and carvings, the photograph was the principal form by which the combatants captured their own images of wartime events. Amateur Allied and Japanese artists were also at work making images of the war—including representations of military encounters with Pacific islanders. These paintings and photographs do more than simply record everyday events in the history of the war on small and distant South Sea islands. In them, we can also discern certain images of self and other that were present in the minds of the makers.

Americans, certainly, came to the Pacific with preconceived ideas about natives. Even though James Michener was still hard at work on his South Pacific tales, Western literature and, more recently, cinema had already inscribed a strong image of Pacific islanders in the minds of many of the servicemen who found themselves "somewhere in the South Pacific." Richard Tregaskis in *Guadalcanal Diary* quotes the surprised reaction of a medical officer traveling on a troop ship. He went below decks, "expecting to find the

Mililat, Papua New Guinea, July 1944.
Islanders look at photographs of themselves displayed outside an Australian Military History Section office. Many had their pictures first taken during the war.
(*Source:* Australian War Memorial.)

Espiritu Santo, Vanuatu (New Hebrides), February 1944.
Along with photographs, servicemen also represented their image of islanders in paintings and drawings. Lt. W. J. Fischer's romanticized portrait of an exotic "native girl" was done for the Navy's Officers Club at Espiritu Santo.
(*Source:* National Archives, U.S. Navy.)

Guadalcanal, Solomon Islands, 1944.
By posing a group of pipe-smoking Solomon Islands women next to a U.S. Women's Reserve recruiting poster, attention is called to the contrast between Western and island images of women.
(*Source:* National Archives, U.S. Marine Corps.)

kids praying, and instead I found 'em doing a native war dance. One of them had a towel for a loin cloth and blacked face, and he was doing a cancan while another beat a tomtom . . ." (Tregaskis 1943, 32).

Such images drew heavily on motifs from the Polynesian Islands. They stressed the physical beauty of both local landscapes and island women. *Time* magazine's issue of June 14, 1943, for example, reported on "seductive Sikaiana"—a Polynesian outlying atoll located deep in the heart of Melanesia. Here, "the South Seas really live up to their literary tradition and the native girls really look like Dorothy Lamour." According to *Time*, military folklore recounted various schemes to get to the island, including "one sea-crashed pilot who was found in his little rubber boat, paddling hotly with his bare hands toward Sikaiana and fighting off rescuers." Similar images of "natural beauty" in the Pacific dominate paintings of local women that adorned mess halls, officers clubs, and the fuselages of warplanes.

As the *Time* magazine account of Sikaiana makes clear, American images of island women extended familiar notions of romance and beauty into exotic settings (where, presumably, normal inhibitions did not apply). But the mythic stories of Sikaiana were an exception. It was more often the case that romanticized images of South Seas were far off the mark.

Although many servicemen found themselves in the Micronesian islands of the North Pacific, or in Polynesian Samoa, Tahiti, or Tonga, most encountered islanders in Melanesia. Here, the image of the other was somewhat darker. Instead of romanticized native girls, military artists burlesqued their

Below, left: **Santa Ana, Solomon Islands, 1943. Whereas the military represented islanders in photographs and paintings, islanders incorporated their own images of the Japanese and the Allies in carvings, weavings, songs, stories, and in dramatic skits. During a village initiation ceremony attended by Allied officers, an effigy of a Japanese soldier—carved out of wood and dressed for the occasion—is used to depict suffering under their occupation.** (*Source:* Auckland Institute and Museum.)

Below, right: **Santa Ana, Solomon Islands, 1943. A carved representation of a Japanese soldier produced for Allies and islanders.** (*Source:* Auckland Institute and Museum.)

Majuro, Marshall Islands, May 1944.
Island images of military outsiders were shaped by American films and magazines that flooded the Pacific during the war. Magazines with sections of photographs were an especially big hit with these Micronesian children, as they were with islanders across the Pacific.
(*Source:* National Archives, U.S. Navy.)

representations of islanders, or parodied the received notion of South Seas beauty in cartoons of local women entitled "As Hollywood sees her, but we've got ringside seats." A photograph taken on Guadalcanal also captures something of this parody: it pictures Cpl. Luigi Greasso dressed in a grass skirt and beads in order to show local villagers "what a Hollywood native looks like." Other prewar themes contributed to images of Melanesians. The men of the Solomon Islands Labour Corps, for example, who carried supplies to Mount Austin during the battle for Guadalcanal, were nicknamed the "Cannibal Battalion."

The war upset preconceived notions about outsiders among islanders, as well as among incoming troops. Prewar understandings of colonists, and relations of inequality between European masters and island servants, unraveled following the onslaught of the Japanese (proposing their Greater East Asia Co-prosperity Sphere), the retreat of the European colonials, and the deluge of Allied troops into the Pacific. The films and magazines that the forces imported into the region also had an impact upon islanders, so much so that one British consultant in the Solomons proposed, "Several thousands of copies of official publications describing the British war effort, as well as large numbers of such journals as *Illustrated London News* might be distributed to counteract the effect of *Life* and other American magazines now [1943] so much in evidence."

Whether Japanese or American, the military outsider now frequently took on an image of a brother. Shared kinship is important in Pacific cultures. It is a basis of mutual support and common goals, even if older and younger brothers stand on slightly unequal footing. The extension of the kin category "brother" to outsiders bespeaks important changes in the local image of others. We hear this in the recollections of now elderly men in Vanuatu who remember that when the Americans went home, they told people, "Don't feel bad. Sometime we'll come again in peace. We'll be brothers; we'll have good times." We see this also in the action of Pouvanaa of Tahiti, who unsuccessfully sought American assistance in his political struggles with the French administration. And we see it in the postwar Maasina Rule (or "brotherhood") movement in the Solomon Islands that also challenged colonialist authority, based in part on recollections of warm wartime relations with military newcomers (Laracy 1983).

These changing images of outsiders, effected by the arrival of Japanese, American, Australian, and other troops, turned back to influence the images islanders had of themselves. As brothers, as equals, islanders could justify their demands to retake control of their own homelands, and to acquire some

Houailou, New Caledonia, November 1944.
The films that circulated in great numbers during the war introduced many islanders to new and more graphic images of Western culture. Here New Caledonian children and their parents are enraptured seeing their first movie, *King of Kings*, portraying the life of Jesus Christ. The film was brought to their mission station by a U.S. military chaplain. (*Source:* National Archives, U.S. Army Signal Corps.)

of the benefits of the modern world economy. In the Pacific, as in colonial areas around the world, the war impelled movement toward independence. These eventually culminated in the political emancipation of most of the region's colonies in the 1960s, 1970s, and 1980s.

In wartime encounters, the images that Europeans held of Pacific islanders also shifted, although perhaps less profoundly. In Papua New Guinea, the tremendous efforts made by carriers and stretcher-bearers for the wounded on the Kokoda Trail rewrote earlier images of islanders as "primitives" or even "savages." Instead, in the words of a maudlin song-poem popular at the time, they became "fuzzy wuzzy angels." A journalist, twenty years later, took note of this improved (if still distorted) image: "The speed with which the public image of a New Guinean was transmogrified from that of a bloodthirsty cannibal with a bone through his nose to that of a dusky-skinned, mop headed, sexless Florence Nightingale must forever remain an inspiration to political propagandists." Nevertheless, shifts in colonialist images of their erstwhile subjects also contributed to postwar realignments in Pacific political relations.

We can observe something of these changing images of islanders in a final pair of photographic poses. These are photographic images of the *making* of photographs. Each captures military photographers in the act of taking a picture of an island scene. Although both were taken in October, 1942, in Samoa, they present very different images of islanders. In the one, we see Marine photographers posing a young Samoan man as "native." He stands in a stream,

Popondetta, Papua New Guinea, April 1982.
In addition to representing prevailing images of Pacific islanders, war photographs also altered those images. A generation after the war's end, Raphael Oimbari with his family holds up one of the war's most famous photographs. Published in *Life*, it depicts Oimbari helping a dying Australian soldier walk to an Army hospital. In these new images of war, "primitive natives" are reposed as "fuzzy wuzzy angels."
(*Source: Sydney Morning Herald.*)

American Samoa, October 1942.
Old and new Pacific images clash as an islander is posed as "native." The duty of military photographers was to document life and war in the islands. When reality was not exactly as expected (as in the stereotype of fierce, spear-throwing natives), it was necessary to do some casting. Here Samoan Marine Tupolie steps out of uniform to please Marine Corps public relations officers.
(*Source:* National Archives, U.S. Marine Corps.)

American Samoa, October 1942.
The war's new islanders: Samoan Marines pose with their rifles for American military photographers and moviemakers.
(*Source:* National Archives, U.S. Marine Corps.)

shirt off, flowered lavalava wrapped around his loins, apparently ready to throw his fishing spear directly at the camera. In the second photograph, we see a changed image. Samoan Marines stand in military formation, wearing white t-shirts and hats, each with a rifle at his side. Three filmmakers make ready to capture the pose. The rifle, here, replaces the traditional spear.

Looking at all of the photographs collected in this volume, these contrasting poses might be kept in mind. During the war, poses—images—of islanders shifted, if only gently. "Native with spear" was reposed as "loyal native volunteer." "Island cannibal" was reposed as "Marine with gun." Each photograph has many, shifting readings. Each freezes an instant in time: an image of a particular historical encounter between islanders and outsiders during one day of the war. Each also presents more general cultural images of military selves relating to exotic island others—shifting images of self and other that the war did much to transform.

Bibliography

This photoessay grows out of several years' research into the ethnohistory of the Pacific War. In addition to photographic archives, we have drawn upon published histories of the war, Pacific ethnographies, unpublished material in military historical archives, and oral historical data that we and others have collected. We use facts, figures, stories, and songs from all these sources in each section of the book. For ease of presentation and reading, however, only published sources are cited. Readers who want to follow up any of the statements or examples we give from unpublished sources may contact us at the East-West Center, Honolulu, HI 96848. We will be happy to provide the source in question. We list in this bibliography the more important material about islander wartime experiences on which we have relied.

Akin, David. 1988. "World War II and the Evolution of Pacific Art." *Pacific Arts Newsletter* 27:5–11.

Alvarado, Manuel. 1980. "Photographs and Narrativity." *Screen Education* 32/33:1–10.

Banta, Melissa, and Curtis M. Hinsley. 1986. *From Site to Sight: Anthropology, Photography, and the Power of Imagery*. Cambridge, Mass.: Peabody Museum Press.

Barrett, Don. 1969. "The Pacific Islands Regiment." In *The History of Melanesia. Second Waigani Seminar*, pp. 493–502. Canberra: ANU Research School of Pacific Studies; Port Moresby: University of Papua New Guinea.

Bennett, Judith A. 1987. *Wealth of the Solomons: A History of a Pacific Archipelago, 1800–1978*. Pacific Islands Monograph Series no. 3. Honolulu: University of Hawaii Press.

Blackman, Margaret B. 1981. *Window on the Past: The Photographic Ethnohistory of the Northern and Kaigani Haida*. Canadian Ethnology Service, Paper 74. Ottawa: National Museum of Canada.

Boutilier, James. 1989. "Kennedy's 'Army': Solomon Islanders at War, 1942–1943." In White and Lindstrom, pp. 329–52.

Budd, Ken. 1989. Letter. *Guadalcanal Echoes* (April): 19.

Butler, Fred A. 1943. "Malaria Control Program on a South Pacific Base." *U.S. Naval Medical Bulletin* 41:1603–12.

Byers, Paul. 1966. "Cameras Don't Take Pictures." *Columbia University Forum* 9(1):27–33.

Carucci, Laurence M. 1989. "The Source of the Force in Marshallese Cosmology." In White and Lindstrom, pp. 73–96.

Chapman, Wilbert McLeod. 1949. *Fishing in Troubled Waters.* Philadelphia: J. B. Lippincott Co.

[Cooper, Harold.] 1946. *Among Those Present: The Official Story of the Pacific Islands at War.* Central Office of Information. London: Her Majesty's Stationery Office.

Counts, David. 1989. "Shadows of War: Changing Remembrance through Twenty Years in New Britain." In White and Lindstrom, pp. 187–203.

Danielsson, Bengt, and Marie Thérèse Danielsson. 1977. *Mururoa Mon Amour.* New York: Penguin.

DeForge, Gerald T. 1981. *Navy Photographer's Mate,* Training series, Module 1, Naval Photography. Navedtra 373-01-00-81. Washington, D.C.: Department of the Navy, Chief of Naval Education and Training.

Divine, David. 1950. *The King of Fassarai.* New York: Macmillan.

Donner, William W. 1989. "'Far Away' and 'Close Up': World War II and Sikarana Perceptions of Their Place in the World." In White and Lindstrom, pp. 149–65.

Edom, Clifton C. 1947. "Photo-Propaganda: The History of Its Development." *Journalism Quarterly* 24:221–26, 238.

Fabian, Rainer, and Hans Christian Adam. 1983. *Images of War: 130 Years of Photography.* Sevenoaks, Kent: New English Library.

Fahey, James J. 1963. *Pacific War Diary: 1942–1945.* New York: Kensington.

Falgout, Suzanne. 1989. "From Passive Pawns to Political Strategists: Wartime Lessons for the People of Pohnpei." In White and Lindstrom, pp. 279–97.

Feldt, Eric A. 1946. *The Coast Watchers.* Oxford: Oxford University Press.

Fox, Charles E. 1962. *Kakamora.* London: Hodder and Stoughton.

Garrison, Ritchie. 1983. *Task Force 9156 and III Island Command: A Story of a South Pacific Advanced Base During World War II, Efate, New Hebrides.* Boston: Nimrod Press.

Gesch, Patrick F. 1985. *Initiative and Initiation.* St. Augustin, W. Germany: Anthropos-Institut.

Geslin, Yves. 1956. "Les Américains aux Nouvelles-Hébrides." *Journal de la Société des Océanistes* 12:245–86.

Gewertz, Deborah. 1983. *Sepik River Societies: A Historical Ethnography of the Chambri and Their Neighbors.* New Haven: Yale University Press.

Guiart, Jean. 1951. "Forerunners of Melanesian Nationalism." *Oceania* 22:81–90.

Gwero, James. 1988. "Oral Histories of World War II from Northern Vanuatu." *'O'o: A Journal of Solomon Islands Studies* 4:37–43.

Halsey, William F., and J. Bryan. 1947. *Admiral Halsey's Story.* New York: McGraw-Hill.

Heinl, R. D. 1944. "Palms and Planes in the New Hebrides." *National Geographic* 86:229–56.

Henrich, Ruth. 1944. *South Sea Epic: War and the Church in New Guinea.* London: Society for the Propagation of the Gospel.

Higuchi, Wakako. 1984. "Micronesian Warriors." *Pacific Daily News* (29 July): 3–4.

———. 1986. "Micronesians and the Pacific War: The Palauans." In *An Oral Historiography of the Japanese Administration in Palau,* D. Ballendorf et al., eds. Report submitted to the Japan Foundation. Agana: Micronesian Area Research Center.

Horton, D. C. 1970. *Fire Over the Islands: The Coast Watchers of the Solomons.* Sydney: A. H. and A. W. Reed.

Inglis, K. S. 1969. "War, Race and Loyalty in New Guinea, 1939–1945." In *The History of Melanesia. Second Waigani Seminar,* pp. 503–30. Canberra: ANU Research School of Pacific Studies; Port Moresby: University of Papua New Guinea.

Kais, K. 1974. Interview with William Metpi. *Oral History* 4:2–36.

Keeble, Andrew, ed. 1980. "World War II in the Solomons: Some Solomon Island Interpretations." Oral History Research Group Report No. 1. Honiara: Solomon Islands Teachers' College.

Koch, Klaus-Friedrich, ed. 1978. *Logs in the Current of the Sea.* Canberra: Australian National University Press.

Kozloff, Max. 1987. *The Privileged Eye: Essays on Photography.* Albuquerque: University of New Mexico Press.

Laracy, Hugh, ed. 1983. *Pacific Protest: The Maasina Rule Movement, Solomon Islands, 1944–1952.* Suva: Institute of Pacific Studies.

Laracy, Hugh, and Geoffrey M. White, eds. 1988. "*Taem Blong Faet:* World War II in Melanesia." *'O'o: A Journal of Solomon Islands Studies* 4. Honiara: USP Centre.

Lawrence, Peter. 1964. *"Road Belong Cargo": A Study of the Cargo Movement in the Southern Madang District New Guinea.* Melbourne: Melbourne University Press.

Leadley, Alan. 1976. "A History of the Japanese Occupation of the New Guinea Islands, and Its Effects, with Special Reference to the Tolai People of the Gazelle Peninsula." Unpublished M.A. thesis, University of Papua New Guinea.

Lepowsky, Maria. 1989. "Soldiers and Spirits: The Impact of World War II on a Coral Sea Island." In White and Lindstrom, pp. 205–30.

Lewinski, Jorge. 1978. *The Camera at War: A History of War Photography from 1848 to the Present Day.* New York: Simon and Schuster.

Lincoln, Satoko. 1979. "Japanese Schools in New Guinea, Papua New Guinea, During the Pacific War, 1942–1945." Unpublished manuscript. University of Hawaii Library.

Lindstrom, Lamont. 1979. "Americans on Tanna: An Essay from the Field." *Canberra Anthropology* 2(2):37–46.

———. 1981. "Cult and Culture: American Dreams in Vanuatu." *Pacific Studies* 4:101–23.

Lord, Walter. 1977. *Lonely Vigil: Coastwatchers of the Solomons.* New York: Viking Press.

Macquarrie, Hector. 1948. *Vouza and the Solomon Islands.* New York: Macmillan.

Manchester, William. 1979. *Goodbye, Darkness: A Memoir of the Pacific War.* New York: Dell.

Mead, Margaret. 1956. *New Lives for Old: Cultural Transformations—Manus 1928–1953.* New York: Dell.

Mead, S. M. 1973. "The Last Initiation Ceremony at Gupuna Santa Ana, Eastern Solomon Islands." *Record of the Auckland Institute and Museum* 10:69–95.

Michener, James A. 1947. *Tales of the South Pacific.* New York: Macmillan.

Moeller, Susan D. 1989. *Shooting War: Photography and the American Experience of Combat.* New York: Basic Books.

Moyes, Norman Barr. 1966. "Major Photographers and the Development of Still Photography in Major American Wars." Ph.D. dissertation, Syracuse University.

Murray, M. 1967. *Hunted: A Coastwatcher's Story.* Adelaide: Rigby Ltd.

Nelson, Hank. 1980a. "*As Bilong Soldia:* The Raising of the Papuan Infantry Battalion in 1940." *Yagl-Ambu* 7:19–24.

———. 1980b. "*Taim Bilong Pait:* The Impact of the Second World War on Papua New Guinea." In *Southeast Asia under Japanese Occupation,* A. W. McCoy, ed., pp. 246–66. New Haven: Yale University Southeast Asia Studies.

———. 1982. *"Taim Bilong Masta": The Australian Involvement with Papua New Guinea.* Sydney: Australian Broadcasting Commission.

Ngwadili, Gafu, David Gegeo, and Karen Watson-Gegeo. 1988. "Malaita Refuge, Guadalcanal Labour Corps." In *The Big Death: Solomon Islanders Remember World War II,* G. White et al., eds., pp. 197–215. Suva: Institute of Pacific Studies.

Oliver, Douglas L. 1961. *The Pacific Islands,* revised edition. New York: Anchor Books.

Osifelo, Sir Frederick. 1985. *Kanaka Boy: An Autobiography.* Suva: Institute of Pacific Studies.

Palomo, Tony. 1984. *An Island in Agony.* Agana: privately printed.

Parsons, Robert F. 1945. *Mob 3: A Naval Hospital in a South Sea Jungle.* New York: Bobbs-Merrill.

Paul, Anthony M. 1974. "A Tale of the South Pacific: Tanna, in the New Hebrides, Awaits Messiah from U.S." *Asia Magazine* (17 November): 3–10.

Peattie, Mark R. 1988. *Nan'yo: The Rise and Fall of the Japanese in Micronesia, 1885–1945.* Pacific Island Monograph Series No. 4. Honolulu: University of Hawaii Press.

Phillips, Christopher. 1981. *Steichen at War.* New York: Harry N. Abrams.

Phillips, N. C. 1957. *Official History of New Zealand in the Second World War 1939–45: Italy, Vol. 1.* Wellington: Department of Internal Affairs.

Ravuvu, Asesela. 1974. *Fijians at War.* Suva: Institute of Pacific Studies.

Read, Kenneth E. 1947. "Effects of the Pacific War in the Markham Valley, New Guinea." *Oceania* 18:95–116.

Rhoades, F. A. 1982. *Diary of a Coastwatcher in the Solomons.* Fredericksburg, Tex.: Admiral Nimitz Foundation.

Robinson, Neville K. 1981. *Villagers at War: Some Papua New Guinea Experiences in World War II.* Pacific Research Monograph No. 2. Canberra: Australian National University.

Rubinstein, Joseph. 1981. "Photographic Facts: False Realities." *Dialectical Anthropology* 5:341–49.

Ryan, Peter. 1960. *Fear Drive My Feet.* Melbourne: Melbourne Paperbacks.

———. 1969. "The Australian New Guinea Administrative Unit (ANGAU)." In *The History of Melanesia. Second Waigani Seminar,* pp. 531–48. Canberra: ANU Research School of Pacific Studies; Port Moresby: University of Papua New Guinea.

Scherer, Joanna Cohan. 1975. "Pictures as Documents: Resources for the Study of North American Ethnohistory." *Studies in the Anthropology of Visual Communication* 2:65–66.

Schütz, Albert J. 1968. *Nguna Texts: A Collection of Traditional and Modern Narratives from the Central New Hebrides.* Honolulu: University of Hawaii Press.

Sesiguo, Arenao K. 1977. "Life Story of Kamuna Hura as a Policeman." *Yagl-Ambu* 4:221–32.

Sigob, Somu. 1975. "The Story of My Life." *Gigibori* 2(1):32–36.

Somare, Michael. 1970. "In a Japanese School." *Journal of the Papua and New Guinea Society* 4:29–32.

———. 1975. *Sana: An Autobiography.* Port Moresby: Niugini Press.

Sontag, Susan. 1977. *On Photography.* New York: Farrar, Straus and Giroux.

Stauffer, Alvin P. 1956. *United States Army in World War II, The Technical Services, The Quartermaster Corps: Operations in the War against Japan.* Washington, D.C.: Office of the Chief of Military History, Dept. of the Army.

Steichen, Edward. 1945. *Power in the Pacific: Official U.S. Navy, Marine Corps and Coast Guard Photographs Exhibited at the Museum of Modern Art, New York: A Pictorial Record of Navy Combat Operations on Land, Sea and in the Sky.* New York: U.S. Camera.

Terkel, Studs. 1984. *"The Good War": An Oral History of World War II.* New York: Pantheon.

Thompson, George Raynor, and Dixie R. Harris. 1966. *United States Army in World War II, The Technical Services, The Signal Corps: The Outcome (Mid-1943 through 1945).* Washington, D.C.: Office of the Chief of Military History, Dept. of the Army.

Thompson, George Raynor, Dixie R. Harris, Pauline M. Oakes, and Dulany Terrett. 1957. *United States Army in World War II, The Technical Services, The Signal Corps: The Test (December 1941 to July 1943).* Washington, D.C.: Office of the Chief of Military History, Dept. of the Army.

Tillman, Frank. 1986. "The Past Pictured: Photographic and Electronic Images as History." Unpublished ms.

Time. 1943. "Seductive Sikaiana." *Time* 41 (24 June): 38, 40.

Trachtenberg, Alan. 1985. "Albums of War: On Reading Civil War Photographs." *Representations* 9:1–32.

Tregaskis, Richard. 1943. *Guadalcanal Diary.* New York: Random House.

Tuzin, Donald. 1983. "Cannibalism and Arapesh Cosmology." In *The Ethnography of Cannibalism*, P. Brown and D. Tuzin, eds., pp. 61–71. Washington, D.C.: Society for Psychological Anthropology.

Van Dusen, Henry P. 1945. *They Found the Church There: The Armed Forces Discover Christian Missions.* New York: Scribner's.

Waiko, John D. 1986. "Oral Traditions among the Binandere: Problems of Method in a Melanesian Society." *Journal of Pacific History* 21:21–38.

———. 1988. "Damp Soil My Bed; Rotten Log My Pillow: A Villager's Experience of the Japanese Invasion." *'O'o: A Journal of Solomon Islands Studies* 4:45–59.

Walker, Allan S. 1957. *Australia in the War of 1939–1945, Medical Series, The Island Campaigns.* Canberra: Australian War Memorial.

Wallace, Paul Jefferson. 1971. *Guinea Gold: History—Port Moresby, Dobodura, Lae, Rabaul, 1942–1946.* Sydney(?): privately printed.

Wallin, H. N. 1967. "The Project Was Roses." *Navy Civil Engineer* (May/June): 16–19; (July): 28–31; (August): 26–28.

War Department. 1945. Combat Photography. Pamphlet No. 11-5. Washington, D.C.: War Office.

Watakabe, Mitsuo. 1972. *Deserted Ponapean Death Band.* Ube City: privately printed.

Weeks, Charles J. 1987. "The United States Occupation of Tonga, 1942–1945: The Social and Economic Impact." *Pacific Historical Review* 56:399–426.

White, Geoffrey M., David Gegeo, David Akin, and Karen Watson-Gegeo, eds. 1988. *The Big Death: Solomon Islanders Remember World War II.* Suva: Institute of Pacific Studies.

White, Geoffrey M., and Lamont Lindstrom, eds. 1989. *The Pacific Theater: Island Representations of World War II.* Pacific Islands Monograph Series no. 8. Honolulu: University of Hawaii Press.

Worsley, Peter. 1968. *The Trumpet Shall Sound: A Study of "Cargo" Cults in Melanesia,* second augmented edition. New York: Schocken Books.

Zoleveke, Sir Gideon. 1980. *Zoleveke, Man from Choiseul.* Suva: Institute of Pacific Studies.

Place Index

Page numbers for photographs appear in boldface.